THE MAN
WHO LOST
HIS SHADOW

also by John A. Sanford
published by Paulist Press

MINISTRY BURNOUT
HEALING AND WHOLENESS
DREAMS AND HEALING
THE INVISIBLE PARTNERS
THE KINGDOM WITHIN
THE MAN WHO WRESTLED WITH GOD
BETWEEN PEOPLE: COMMUNICATING ONE-TO-ONE

THE MAN
WHO LOST
HIS SHADOW

John A. Sanford

Paulist Press • *New York/Ramsey*

Library of Congress Catalog Card Number: 82-62414

ISBN: 0-8091-0337-0

Published by Paulist Press
545 Island Road, Ramsey, N.J. 07446

Printed and bound in the United States of America

Contents

• *Acknowledgments* •

My thanks to
my wife, Linny,
my sister, Virginia Clark,
my sister-in-law, Diana Sanford,
and to my friends
Robert Johnson, Morton and Barbara Kelsey,
who read this little story and gave me
the benefit of many helpful comments.
Also to Helen Macey,
whose skillful editing made
the final manuscript preparation
possible.

A Strange Encounter

Trucks rumbled by on mysterious night missions and acrid city smells hovered in the fog-damp air as Mark walked despondently down the street. A stray cat appeared momentarily in the light of a street lamp, then scurried out of Mark's way and into the blackness of an alley. In strange contrast a clock on a distant high-rise building announced to anyone who cared that it was almost midnight.

Mark McLaughlin had lived all of his twenty-six years in New York. He loved and hated the city, both oppressive and fascinating, with its cliffs of buildings, and ground of concrete, and lamp-post trees, but now he hardly noticed his surroundings as he was sunk so deeply in the quicksand of his thoughts.

"Caroline, what have you done to me?" he groaned to himself. "In only two weeks we were to be married. But tonight you ended it. Just like that. Oh, you said you had warned me, but I thought you loved me. You told me that you did, you know. Now I'm cast aside like I never meant anything to you.

1

Where did it all go wrong? What will become of me now?"

Mark plunged his face into his hands, hot with tears, then stumbled on the curb as he reached the end of the street. "Goddamn curb," he complained. Then, with hands in his pockets and head down, he walked rapidly the last few blocks toward his apartment. As he rounded a corner he glanced behind him—his eye had been caught by a moving form—and saw, perhaps thirty feet away, a man and woman walking behind him. In the half-darkness he could not see their features clearly, but the man, vaguely middle-aged, appeared to be vital and strong and walked with his head erect, while the woman, who kept a step behind him, had her eyes downcast and was much slighter.

For a moment Mark felt a rush of irrational fear rise up in him, chasing away his dark thoughts; then his fear subsided. "This guy looks threatening but he's got a woman with him. If someone's going to mug you they don't take their woman along."

Having reassured himself, Mark continued on his way, but as his fear disappeared his despondent thoughts returned. He rounded the final corner to his apartment, now only two blocks away. As he did so he saw the man and woman again. They were now the only ones besides himself on the street and were walking half a block behind him, the woman still walking slightly behind the man. "Strange that they're going the same way I am. Maybe they live nearby."

Mark reached the foot of the stairs that led up to a dimly lit hall and the door to the apartment he called home. His shoes clomped loudly as he walked up the uncarpeted, worn wooden steps and gained the landing. "Yesterday I came up these stairs two at a time. Now look at me. I can barely drag myself up them . . . like my feet are made of lead."

He reached the door to his apartment. It seemed to look back at him glumly as he struggled to find his key. At last he found it, put it in the lock, and turned it. The door yielded to his shove, groaning as it turned inward to let him enter.

Mark stepped inside and poked around in the darkness for the room's only lamp and switched it on. College textbooks lay in an untidy heap on the cheap wooden desk. Papers were piled on what passed for the dining room table. A couple of wooden chairs stood around stiffly, and an overstuffed easy chair sat in front of the used black-and-white portable TV. Soiled curtains partly concealed windows that badly needed washing, and a musty smell, that was a composite from the lives of the many people who had lived here over the years, permeated the apartment. An uninspiring picture of a scene with a meadow and cows hung precariously on one wall, and a poster of a rock music group with long hair and outlandish costumes, pinned to the wall with yellow thumb tacks, seemed to challenge it from the wall across the room.

"Early American orange crate," Mark murmured in disgust as he inspected his gloomy surroundings. "She said she was going to help me fix it up. What the hell, I'll get a beer." Mark gave the front door a kick and it slammed shut and locked itself. He found his way into the kitchen, past a table

3

still piled with dirty dishes from breakfast, opened the door to his refrigerator, and peered inside.

"Goddamn," he muttered, as the beer escaped his sight. Then he grunted approvingly as he saw it at last. "Who the hell put it behind the milk?" he complained out loud, though no one lived in the apartment but himself. In a moment the top was off the can and he was about to take the first cool, soothing draught when a sound from the other room caught his attention.

"Anybody there?" he called out in hushed tones, suddenly alert with apprehension. Then, remembering he had shut the door to the apartment, he summoned up the nerve to peer cautiously into the living room. There, to his astonishment, he saw the man and woman whom he had seen walking behind him only a few minutes earlier.

A deep, thousand-year-old instinct came up in Mark, and in a moment he had taken the measure of the two strangers the way a beast in the jungle might size up an unexpected adversary. The man was only slightly taller than average, but he was heavily built, with a square, muscular body. Sharp, strong bones made his face look craggy, like a mountain cliff, and his dark eyes peered with a peculiar intensity from underneath bushy eyebrows. His full, wildly straggling hair matched in unkemptness the unpressed suit that hung like a sack over a powerful body that seemed to emanate vibrations of animal vitality and cunning.

The woman stood a step behind her man, just as she had walked a step behind him on the street. She was slightly built, and perhaps six inches shorter than the man. Her face was plain and colorless, devoid of makeup. Her brown hair was straight and nondescript, and she kept her eyes focused on the floor at Mark's feet. A baggy, sexless gray dress hung down almost to her ankles, concealing whatever contours her body might have had, and she carried an oversized purse. Her plainness reminded Mark of those unidentifiable little brown birds that run around on the grass, and yet, in spite of her plain and birdlike quality, Mark thought he perceived a gleam of shrewdness in her downcast eyes.

For what seemed like an unending moment they all stared at each other. Then Mark's instinctual coolness gave way to fear, as he asked in a voice that quavered, "The door. I thought I shut it. How did you get in? Who are you, and what do you want?"

The strange man smiled, a managed smile that was more like a grimace. But Mark noticed that his steely, dark eyes did not smile; they remained fixed on him as though the man was peering into his soul. "No reason to be afraid," he said in a deep, throaty voice that sounded like gravel being washed along the bottom of a stream bed. "I'm not here to hurt you. In fact, I've come to offer you help."

Mark relaxed slightly. "Help me?" he answered. "Who are you anyway, and how can you help me?"

"Of course you want to know who I am. Call me a dealer if you like. I deal in what people want, and I try to see to it that they get it. That's why I'm here now. This woman here," he gestured with his hand toward the woman behind him without bothering to turn around, "is my wife."

Mark glanced at the woman, then back at the man. "What makes you think I need help?"

"Oh I know your problem. Such an unfortunate talk you had with Miss Cameron. She's so pretty. A charming lady, really."

"You know Caroline?" Mark asked in disbelief.

The man began to pace back and forth, reminding Mark of a panther in a cage. "I would not say I know her exactly," the man continued, "but I know of her, and I know you, and it was clear from the conversation the two of you just had why she wants nothing more to do with you."

Mark was incredulous. "How do you know what we said?" But before the man could reply Mark's mind was flooded with memories of that recent, disastrous talk, so vivid that he felt transported painfully, suddenly to the events that had taken place earlier in the evening.

He had been in his apartment when Caroline had phoned and asked him to come over. There was a strangely somber tone to her voice on the phone, but Mark ignored it and leaped at the chance to see her, as he always did. "Maybe she's horny and wants to go to bed," he thought hopefully. "She's damn good in bed!" So he had arrived at her warm and well-appointed apartment full of good cheer and plunked himself down in her comfortable easy chair, his legs sprawled over the arm, and admired his good-looking fiancée.

"Seductive as usual," Mark thought to himself approvingly as his eyes took in her slim body, with its gently rounded breasts, and feminine curves

6

made more alluring by her carefully chosen colorful pink sweater. Her long brown hair hung loosely in just that careless manner that Mark found so attractive. Her slender ankles seemed all the more appealing as she sat in stockinged feet, her shoes carelessly kicked off under the chair. As always she made Mark think of homemade bread being baked in the oven, picnics in the park, and balmy summer nights under a full moon.

Mark said brightly, "Glad you called. I was lonely."

Caroline let her gaze fall to the floor, then lifted it again to look at him directly with her brown eyes slightly moistened with tears. She dispensed with formalities. "I can't go through with it."

"What do you mean you can't go through with it?" Mark said, suddenly suspicious.

"I can't go through with our wedding."

It was as though a wet fish had been thrown in his face. "You're joking, of course."

"It's no joke. I'm going to call Father Murray tomorrow and tell him it's off." Caroline's eyes welled up with tears, and yet, though she spoke softly, she spoke firmly like someone who had gone through a great struggle and had finally made up her mind.

"Caroline, what are you talking about? What happened? Don't you love me?"

"It's not that I don't love you, but too many things are wrong."

"Nothing's wrong. I love you, don't I?"

"Do you? It seems to me if you did you wouldn't live the way you do."

"What's wrong with how I live?"

"I've told you before, but nothing changes."

"Well tell me again," Mark said, beginning to feel belligerent.

"Well, look at what you owe. You borrow from everybody, even our friends."

"There you go again, exaggerating. I don't borrow from *everybody*. You must mean the money I borrowed from Joan and Freddie. I'll pay it back soon."

"It's been six months already."

"Well, it's not like I'm rich you know."

"That's another problem. You still don't have a job. You don't work."

"How can I work when I'm in college? Do you want me to get some piddly little job and waste my time?"

Caroline's eyes flashed, "Well I have a piddly little job, don't I? Typing somebody else's letters in a miserable office every day. But you, you've been going to college for eight years now. You're twenty-six years old and still you're going to college. And you told me last year that you would finish and get a job before we married."

"I've been looking."

"Looking! You're always looking. If you want to look, then look at our life together. Do you ever take me out to dinner? No, you can never afford it. I always make the dinner, and we eat here."

"Is that what you want then—for me to take you out to dinner? Is that the whole problem?"

Her gaze softened again. "It's not that I need to go out, but it makes me lose faith in you. You do exactly as you please and expect the world to take care

8

of you. I admit that sometimes I like taking care of you. But when I'm married it'll be different with me. I'll want you to take care of me then. I want children, you know."

"I told you that I want children too."

"Am I supposed to support them?" Caroline asked accusingly.

Mark fell silent. The clock on the mantel nearby ticked away the seconds and then he said in a lowered voice, "Then why did you go with me this long? Why did you agree to marry me in the first place? Don't you realize how you're hurting me?"

The tears were streaming down her face now. "I know I'm hurting you, Mark, and I know I'm hurting myself. Do you think this is easy for me? I've agonized for weeks over this. I do love you, Mark, don't you see? I love your sense of life. I love the way you walk, and the way you wave your hands when you talk. I like your funny jokes, and the way you can make me laugh. You're fun to be with, when you aren't in a bad humor, and somehow I've always had faith in you. Until now."

"So you love me but you can't marry me. Then maybe we can postpone the wedding. Okay? You wait and see. I'll change, and then we'll get married."

"No, Mark, that won't do. You've told me that before. It was always, 'Wait, you'll see, I'll change.' Well, I can't wait any longer. I'm getting older. I have to find someone I can depend on. I need a man, Mark, not a child to take care of. No, I'm going to call the church tomorrow."

Mark argued some more, but it was no use. Car-

9

oline, who often seemed so tender and yielding, could also be strong and firm. They both cried, but when at last Mark left, Caroline had not changed her mind. The last he saw of her, she was standing at the top of the stairs that led to her apartment, her hair disheveled now, and her pretty sweater wet with tears, watching him as he walked away.

The memory of that dreadful talk with Caroline receded as quickly as it had come, and Mark was once more back in his apartment with the stranger, though his wife seemed to have disappeared.

Mark asked suspiciously, "How do you know these things?"

The intruder tried to speak soothingly, but his piercing eyes spoke another language. "It's not important how I know these things. What is important is that I know how unhappy you are and can offer a solution."

"You can?"

"Yes, I'm prepared to leave with you a considerable sum of money, more money than you could make if you worked for years. And work, you'll remember, is not something you like. It's money enough so that a clever person like you can persuade a willing woman like Caroline to believe that you have a job and that you've changed. You can pay off your debts and take your young lady out to dinner every night for months if you like. And in return I ask for practically nothing."

"Come on now. Even I know you don't get something for nothing."

"You're doubtful, of course. But you're also intrigued, aren't you? I can tell by the look on your face that you want the money."

The man motioned to his wife, who had silently reappeared and stood behind him as before. She reached into her enormous purse and handed him a thick stack of green bills. The man undid the bundle and began to count out the bills as he placed them on the table. "One hundred ... one thousand ... five thousand ... There! Fifty thousand dollars! You've never seen so much money in your life have you?"

"Let me see those!" Mark cried. The man moved aside and Mark inspected the money. Then he turned to the man and said: "You're serious!"

"Now you're coming around."

"What do you want from me?"

"Something so insignificant that no one will even notice you without it. All I want from you is your shadow."

"My shadow! You can't be serious. You mean *this* shadow?" He pointed to the shadow silhouetted on the floor by the light of the lamp.

"Yes, that shadow. You wonder why? I guess you could say I collect shadows. It's a peculiarity of mine. Furthermore, I know how to separate a person and his shadow. It's quite harmless. No pain at all. You won't even notice anything has happened. All this money in exchange for something you never even notice. What could be a better bargain than that?"

"But wouldn't I feel strange without a shadow?"

11

The man laughed. "How often do you think about your shadow now? Do you think you would care if it wasn't there?"

"But other people will notice."

"Do you go around looking at their shadows? Come now, who looks at shadows? I can promise you absolutely that when I am done no one will notice you and say, 'Look, that man's shadow is gone.'"

Mark snorted in disbelief. "Okay, if you can take my shadow away from me it's a deal."

"It's agreed, then," the man said. Suddenly he was all action, like a beast of prey who has been carefully waiting and now springs for his victim. He pulled some papers from his coat pocket and smoothed them out on the table. "Merely sign these, please, and we'll go right to work."

Mark looked at the papers. The writing on them was illegible—or was it written in some foreign language? For whatever reason, Mark had trouble reading it, but he could make out the words "shadow . . . exchange . . . money." Then he felt a terrific repulsion come up in him. It was as though his thousand-year-old instinct was working again, perhaps trying to warn him of some incredible danger. But he also felt his resistance melt like ice cream on a hot summer day. The animal vitality of the stranger seemed to overwhelm him and he heard himself saying, "It's some kind of joke, but what the hell—for this much money I'll sign."

Mark reached for his pen, but the man interrupted him. "No, use this pen. It must be signed in blood. It's the Law, you see."

"The Law?" Mark asked numbly, for it was as though he had lost his will.

The man ignored his question. "Here, I'll show you."

In a twinkling the man had nicked Mark's arm neatly with a small knife he suddenly produced from his pocket. The blood trickled down toward Mark's hand.

"Damn it, what are you doing?" Mark cried, offended and frightened.

But the man did not hesitate. Mark felt like a log being swept downstream as the stranger dipped his pen in Mark's blood and handed it to him. Mark signed. "Two copies," the man demanded. Mark signed the second copy.

"Now," the man commanded, "merely stand there in the light. Bad light you have in this place, but it will do. Let the lamp be in front of you so the shadow is behind. Then there won't be any difficulty."

Mark did as he was told. The man now marched around in a counter-clockwise direction twelve times, then reversed himself and went around him a thirteenth time in the opposite direction. The woman opened her cavernous purse again and the man seemed to drop something inside.

"There, you see," he said. "No pain. You didn't feel a thing. I'll be going. The money is yours."

"But wait, you didn't sign."

"There's no need for me to sign. I always keep my bargain. You're the only one who can't be trusted."

13

Mark started to speak again, but with remarkable agility for such a big man the mysterious intruder and his plain little wife had disappeared out the door. Just for one moment the woman cast a quick look behind her at Mark as though she wanted to say something. Then they were gone.

As soon as the man was gone Mark felt released, more like himself. He went over to the table. The money was all there. He ran his hands through it and counted it again and again. As he reveled in the cash any doubts he had about his bargain disappeared.

"So much for so little," he said out loud to himself. "Now I can make Caroline come back to me."

His eye fell on the contract lying on the table. Mark saw where he had written his name in blood, but the man's name didn't appear on the document. "Strange that he didn't sign. But no matter. He kept his part of the bargain. The money's all here."

It took Mark a long time to fall asleep. His mind kept racing over the events of the evening, happily making plans for the next day. Finally he fell into a fitful sleep, troubled by dreams, as though he was happy on the outside, but unhappy on the inside.

The Awful Truth

Mark woke to the sounds of the city stirring to life. Light from the sun already high in the sky managed to struggle through the haze of the city and the unwashed windows of his apartment to brighten his bedroom. Mark usually slept as late as possible because he hated the mornings with the responsibilities they brought him, but this morning he leaped out of bed energetically and hurried to the living room where the money had been left the evening before.

He danced a little jig of happiness as he exclaimed aloud, "It's still here; it wasn't a dream. This is the day my life will be different forever!"

Perhaps because he had lived alone for so long, Mark often talked to himself. "Have to look my best today," he found himself saying as he made his way to the bathroom. "Got to make plans. First get some new clothes, the kind Caroline likes me to wear. Then I'll pay Joan and Freddie back the money I owe—well, part of it anyway. They may never recover from the shock! Then I'll make a reservation

15

for two at a restaurant for dinner—a good restaurant, but not too fancy. Don't want Caroline to get suspicious about how I got the money. I'll have to come up with some story she'll believe. I'll tell her there's a surprise for her, that I've got a job after all, that I've had it all along but wanted to wait for my first pay check to surprise her. She'll believe me because she wants to believe me, and the money with me will be convincing. All I've got to do is persuade her to come to dinner with me so I can talk with her. From there on it will be clear sailing."

Mark was in the bathroom. He picked up one of the towels that were scattered on the floor like leaves on the ground, and reached for the shaving gear in the cabinet over the basin. Then he stared in disbelief. The mirror that should have been on the cabinet door was gone. "What the hell's happened to the goddamn mirror?" Mark muttered in irritated wonder.

He looked everywhere but couldn't find it. Finally he had to conclude that the man and his wife must have taken it the night before. He remembered that the woman disappeared briefly. She must have come into the bathroom and put the mirror into the cavernous purse she carried. Why would she want a cheap old mirror? No matter. If her thing was having to take mirrors, Mark could do without it. He'd shave without a mirror this morning and buy another one later on. After all, he had lots of money now.

The momentary dark cloud that the disappearance of the mirror had cast on Mark's exuberant mood left and his joyful mood returned. In a few minutes he was dressed and ready for the outside world and his new life. He stopped by the living room table and slipped a fistful of bills into his wallet and pockets. He opened the groaning door to leave but suddenly thought of his shadow.

Mark stepped back into the room, turned on the lamp, and stood squarely in its light. He looked down at the floor where his shadow should have been. There was nothing to be seen. The man really must have taken it with him, Mark concluded, but, as he said, who would notice? Mark reflected that he wouldn't have noticed it himself if he hadn't made it a point to look. As the man said, who needs a shadow?

Mark left the apartment, slamming the door behind him. He raced down the stairs two at a time, jumping over the last steps to land on the sidewalk with a thud. Then he walked briskly down the bustling, clanging street.

At this hour of the morning people buzzed around the streets like bees in a hive, and cars and trucks honked and roared their way complainingly to their various destinations. The entrance to the subway was across the street, so Mark hurried to the corner of the intersection. The light was green for him, but cars were turning right and he waited impatiently for a break in the traffic. Then, remembering that he had the right of way, he damned the cars for ignoring him, decided that he would make them stop for him, and stepped out into the street, confidently sure that the next car that wanted to turn right would stop and let him go by. But to his shocked surprise the car didn't pause; in fact, the driver seemed to be aiming his car right at him.

"Hey, you bastard, where do you think you're going?" Mark cried out loud as he leaped out of the way of the lethal car. The driver did not even glance at him, but plowed on down the street unrepentantly.

"Got to get out of this city," Mark muttered. "People here get worse all the time, always hurrying and paying no attention where they're going."

On the other side of the street Mark began to make his way through the bustling crowd to the subway entrance. A big black man came striding along from Mark's right and Mark paused so the man could go around him. But the black man did not go around. Like a juggernaut he hit Mark a powerful blow with his shoulder that sent him reeling. Mark fell backward right into the side of a nattily dressed businessman, bounced off him, and fell to the pavement. Before he could even cry out another man came hurrying along and Mark watched incredulously as this man walked right over him.

From where he had fallen, Mark cried out at the men who had treated him so shamefully, "Why don't you watch where you're going?" But the men never turned around as they hurried down the street.

Mark picked himself up off the sidewalk, darted to the subway entrance, and started down the stairs. His earlier exuberance had been dampened by the accidents, but was now slowly returning as he made his way toward the people who were jammed up at the subway turnstile. He joined the line, behind a woman carrying an umbrella over her shoulder. Suddenly a stab of pain flashed across Mark's face as the point of the woman's umbrella poked him in the eye. Mark took an involuntary step backward just as the man behind him stepped forward so that his knee gouged Mark painfully in the rear. A moment later another woman appeared from the side and forced her way into the line by simply running into Mark who, off balance as he was, was thrown completely out of the line. He saved himself from falling only by stumbling to the subway wall and leaning against it.

Something was wrong, very wrong. Everyone was acting so strangely. Mark looked at the pushing people trying to get into the subway and felt weak. They were suddenly like maniacs to him. What on earth should he do? He decided that he would eat. Then he would feel strong enough to face them.

The coffee shop was about six blocks away. He wondered whether he should take a cab or walk when a taxi cruised by, empty except for the driver. "With all this money, why should I walk?" he thought to himself. He shouted at the driver and waved his arms, but the cab cruised right past.

"He must be answering a call," Mark explained to himself. "No matter; I'll walk." But walking wasn't so easy with all the people coming at him. Mark soon noticed that he was now instinctively avoiding them and not trusting them to avoid him. He finally reached the coffee shop with a sense of relief. The food was not very good here—the eggs were too greasy and the coffee weak—but the waitress was pretty and always talked to him cheerfully, and he knew some of the other regulars, so the atmosphere was friendly.

He opened the door to the cafe, breathed in the aroma of hot coffee, and welcomed the sounds of clinking dishes, rustling newspapers, and guttural conversation. He found an empty seat at the counter.

The pretty waitress swished past Mark on busy missions. Mark called out a greeting to her, but she did not acknowledge him. When she came past him again Mark said, "I'll take the usual, Beautiful," and smiled his most charming smile. But still she did not respond.

"What's eating her this morning?" he asked himself.

Another customer came in and sat on the empty stool beside Mark. Soon the waitress came up to the stranger and asked him in a friendly way, "Coffee, mister?" The stranger answered, "Sure." In a moment she had poured him a comforting drink of the warm black liquid.

"Hey, how about me?" Mark called. The girl ignored him.

Mark was baffled. She was acting as if he wasn't there at all. In fact everyone was acting as though he didn't exist. Mark wondered if it was some weird game people were playing with him. But why would they do that? Was there something wrong with him? Mark studied his clothes, looked at his hands, ran his fingers through his hair, but everything about him seemed to be as usual. He looked at the floor for his shadow. It was gone, of course, but so what? It was just as the strange man had said: no one had even noticed. But *something* clearly was wrong ... he could feel it. And maybe it was something wrong with him, and not with them. He began to feel unreal, as though he was walking through a desolate landscape, except that in this case the landscape was real and he ... Could it be that he was dreaming? Or could it be that something *worse* had happened?

Suddenly Mark leaped off the counter stool, raced out of the cafe, and hurried down the street. People came at him like linebackers charging a ball carrier, but he dodged them adroitly. He saw a taxi and waved at it, but when it paid no attention to him he hurried on, picking his way through the crowds as though he were walking through a mine field. Once he almost stopped in front of a store with a large glass window, but then he muttered to himself, "No, I must be *sure*," and hurried on again.

When he reached a street intersection he waited impatiently for the light to change, hugging a lamp post so no one would bump into him, and when the light turned green he raced across. On he went through a city that had once been friendly but now seemed like a hostile, uncaring place. Eventually he reached the department store.

Fortunately it was not yet busy. He made his way without incident through the women's shoes and handbag sections, past the neatly dressed, bored looking saleswomen with their name tags pinned over their breasts, and into the men's department. Hardly any customers were there, but the salesmen ignored him. He went up to the full length mirror the store provided for customers. He stood in front of it. What he saw was—nothing.

Mark's heart sank. He moved his body this way and that, but there was no reflection in the mirror. He couldn't see himself! Was that the way it was with other people—they couldn't see him either? Desperately he waved his arms at the mirror, reached out to touch it, even jumped up and down, but the mirror looked back at him blank and empty. Marked realized the awful conclusion: he was invisible! That was why people ran him down on the streets. That was why the taxi driver didn't stop for him and the waitress ignored him. And that was why that infernal little woman stole the mirror from his bathroom. They had tricked him. They knew he would be invisible without his shadow, but didn't want him to find out until they had a chance to get far away. But now he knew the awful truth. In his agony he gasped, "Oh God! Nobody can see me!"

Desperate

Mark stared glumly around his bedroom in the half light of dawn. For a long time after his shocking discovery of the day before he had wandered aimlessly through the city, with no idea at all what to do, hoping that somehow people would be able to see him again. When darkness began to fall he had made his way home, thinking ruefully to himself, "Well, I don't have to worry about getting mugged anyway." When he had finally opened the door to his apartment and stepped inside he was exhausted, but he had slept only fitfully, awakened repeatedly by nightmarish dreams and anxious thoughts. Now, in spite of his unassuaged weariness, he could sleep no more.

He stumbled out of bed. His body ached from the bruises he had received the day before, and his stomach was growling for food, for he had not eaten anything for over twenty-four hours.

Mark realized that, invisible or not, apparently he had to eat. He hated this time of day, and it seemed outlandish to be up and looking for food, but he would have welcomed the dawn with open arms if only he could be seen.

He opened the refrigerator door and peered inside. He looked for the bread, but then remembered it had gone stale and he had thrown it away. He reached for the eggs, but he had eaten the last one two days ago. He picked up a half-full carton of milk, but when he opened it the rank odor of sour milk assaulted him. "Damn refrigerator," he exclaimed as he slammed its door to punish it for what was obviously a personal plot conceived against him. "It's as empty as a beer keg on New Year's Day. For Christ's sake, why didn't I shop earlier? Now what do I do? Starve to death?"

Ten minutes later Mark was warily picking his way along the nearly deserted streets toward the all-night grocery store. It had rained during the night and the air was pleasantly damp. Ordinarily even Mark would have enjoyed such a morning with its fresh, cleansed scent, but today he was oblivious to its beauties as he trudged along, thinking how much easier it was for him to get around when all the sensible people were still home in bed.

Finally he reached the store and approached the front door gingerly. He paused and read the forbidding signs plastered on the glass: *Shoplifters will be prosecuted . . . Electronic surveillance at work . . . Armed Response . . . Use a gun and go to jail.* It wasn't a very hospitable way for a guy in trouble to be greeted, he reflected.

He peered inside. The clerk was at the checkout stand, and two bleary-eyed customers were fishing around on the counters for breakfast items they had neglected to buy at the supermarket the day before. Mark knew there was no use trying to buy food. He would have to steal it. It reminded him of when he was a kid and used to lift comic books. Those were the good old days when they didn't have electronic surveillance. But he wondered what would happen if he took something from the shelves and it registered on the store's infernal detection devices? Or what would happen if the clerk couldn't see Mark but could see a quart of milk Mark was stealing floating away through the air all by itself? He allowed himself a brief, ironic laugh as he wondered how the police would go about fingerprinting an invisible shoplifter.

Now he pushed open the door and slid through, walking cat-carefully. The clerk didn't look up and Mark missed the friendly "Hi" he usually gave his customers as they entered the store; it was a friendly way to be greeted, even though Mark knew the store trained the clerk to say this on the theory that it made people more reluctant to pilfer the place. Stealthily he moved toward the shelves of food, then caught himself, and wondered what he thought he was doing walking around like a thief when no one could see him.

He went boldly to the well-stocked shelves, reached for a loaf of bread, then for some cheese, then into the refrigerator for some milk, looking around warily all the time to see if anyone was coming, and, if so, whether or not they could see the things he was taking. At last a customer rounded the corner and came up the aisle where Mark was standing. Mark froze tensely, clutching his ill-gotten gains, but the man didn't blink an eye. Then Mark knew that whatever he touched was invisible to other people just as he was.

His fear gone, Mark moved rapidly toward the exit. When he was a kid he might have liked to steal like this. Then he could have had all the comic books and candy bars he wanted with no fear of getting caught. But now somehow Mark didn't feel very proud of himself. Outside he paused, reflected for a few moments, then suddenly turned around, re-entered the store, took out a five dollar bill and placed it on the counter. In a moment he was gone again, wondering to himself if the five dollars would be visible to the clerk once he had left. He stole a quick glance behind him to see the surprised clerk picking up the greenback, but then he slipped quickly away still feeling like a thief.

Mark didn't want to go back to his apartment; it was too depressing to be so totally alone. Instead he found his way to Central Park, found a suitable bench and sat down. Even though he was hungry he did not eat right away but waited for people to come and fill the park with their talk and noise, for he could not bear to eat without at least the sight of other human beings around him. Glumly he stared at the ground. Then he became aware of a small, shallow pool of water, left there from the recent rain. He leaned over and gazed into it, hoping against hope that he would see his image reflected. Nothing. It was as though this final disappointment did something to Mark. Hungry, tired, frantic, his mind began to wander and conceive strange fantasies. What if there weren't any people in the whole city who could see their reflection? What if everyone came, stared into the pool of water, and saw nothing? What if he wasn't the only one without a shadow, but all the people had lost their shadows? People walking around invisible to each other ... bumping into each other and getting angry with each other and no one knowing what was the matter ... everyone isolated, separated as he was, all because no one had a shadow ... people looking into mirrors and pretending they could see something, when really they couldn't, but no one wanting to admit it ...

Suddenly, with a wrench of his will, Mark pulled himself out of his fantastic thoughts. No, he was the only one who couldn't be seen. See how other people were beginning to come into the park now? They were talking with each other. Some were even laughing. When they walked along the paths and came to people walking the other way they saw each other and moved aside so each could pass. His thoughts had been close to madness. Much more of that kind of stuff and he would be a raving lunatic and they would come and lock him up—except, of course, no one could hear him. Glumly he began to munch his bread and cheese and gulp down milk, while he watched people walking through the park enjoying themselves in the freshness of the morning and the warmth of the rising sun.

The food helped, and he was beginning to feel slightly more hopeful when a huge woman, with a small, poodle-like dog on a leash, came shuffling bear-like toward the bench where Mark was sitting.

A few feet away the dog sniffed, stared at where Mark was sitting unseen on the bench, and growled as though he were seeing a ghost. "Hush, Pootsie!" the woman said disapprovingly, but the dog hung back and was still growling even as the woman lumbered close to the bench. "Damn!" Mark groaned. He leaped out of the way just before the woman poised herself precariously in front of the bench and then descended like a rockslide on the very spot where he had been sitting.

Mark's spark of hope vanished again. It seemed he wouldn't starve to death, but he couldn't even sit on a park bench without being growled at by the Pootsies of this world, and almost crushed by some female dreadnought. Yet there *must* be a way. Maybe he should see a psychiatrist? But what do you say to a psychiatrist who can't see you and can't hear you? Do you say, "Oh, Doctor, would you please give me one of your visibility pills?" Mark had to think his situation through again.

He pondered: No one could see him, and no one could hear him. When he picked up an object it, too, became invisible, but when he put it down it could be seen again; at least the clerk in the store had seen the five dollar bill he had placed on the counter. It was essential that he be able to communicate with someone. That's it! If what he put down was visible, perhaps he could write out a message and give it to someone. Why hadn't he thought of it before? But who? You couldn't go up to just anyone in a situation like this. It had to be someone who wouldn't be easily frightened. Then he thought of Father Murray. He's the one, Mark reasoned, for he's a priest and used to dealing with the kind of deviltry Mark seemed to have gotten himself into.

The chimes of St. Cyprian's Church were just beginning their noonday serenade when Mark reached the door of the great ivy-covered structure. For one moment he looked down at the ground hoping that in the bright sunlight he would see his shadow once again, but it wasn't there. He was transparent like glass, he thought, but he wasn't through yet.

Mark opened the double doors leading into the parish hall and entered. For a moment he thought he caught a glimpse of a man's figure moving quickly away from him, probably Morris the sexton. He headed for the office of the priest. Usually one could not get past the keen eyes of Father Murray's secretary, who watched over him like the mythical dragon with a thousand eyes that guarded the golden fleece, and who hailed down anyone who came within earshot with a hearty, ringing greeting. But this time, invisible as he was, it was easy for Mark to skip past the buxom lady and make his way to the door of the pastor's study. The door was ajar, and Mark entered Father Murray's spacious room. The priest was a tall, strong-looking man on the youngish side of middle-age. He was as handsome as his oak-paneled office and exuded Christian confidence and good will and churchly authority. He was busy at his desk working on some papers.

Mark's eyes roved around the room looking for what he needed. There it was: paper, and a pen nearby on the desk. Mark reached for them. He knew as soon as he picked them up they would become invisible to the priest. He took them over to a nearby straight chair, sat down, and wrote:

Father Murray:

You must help me! It will seem incredible to you, but I am in this room with you right now. You cannot see me, nor can you hear me, although I can see and hear you. I will explain all of this to you, but first I must contact you. That is why I am writing this note. As long as I hold this paper it is invisible to you, but when I put the paper down it will be visible once again. After I am through writing this message I will put the paper where you can see it. When you read this message I know you will be startled. You will not be able to believe what you read. But please take a chance with me. Let me know you have read the note by calling my name. Unless you do I will be without hope.

Desperately,
Mark McLaughlin

Mark stood up and carefully, fearfully, carried the note to Father Murray's desk. The priest continued to work on his papers, unaware of anything extraordinary taking place. Deftly Mark slipped the paper in front of Father Murray so that it lay on the papers on which he was working, where Mark knew he could not help but see it. Then he stood back a step or two and held his breath waiting for the reaction.

For several moments Father Murray stared at the paper in front of him, while Mark pleaded with his eyes for him to speak. And at last he did speak, "How did this piece of paper get here?" he said to no one in particular. "I was working on my parish report and it wasn't here before. Suddenly it appeared in front of me! How very strange." And the priest looked around the room, sweeping every corner with his eyes to see if anyone else was with him. "Oh well," he finished, and put the paper aside.

Mark's heart sank like lead into the pit of his stomach as he realized what had happened. Father Murray had seen the paper all right, but he had not seen anything Mark had written on it. Glumly Mark realized that not only could he not be seen, but without his shadow he could not make an impression on anything either. It was no use. He couldn't reach the priest. There was no way he could make Father Murray know he was there.

Mark sank back hopelessly into the chair and remained there lost in the quagmire of his dark thoughts until the priest rose from the desk and left the office. Mark heard him call to his secretary, "I'm going to lunch with Father Peters. If you need me, I'll be back about two o'clock."

What a wonderful sound, Mark reflected. How grand it was to be able to say to someone, "I'm going to lunch and will be back about two o'clock." Mark would have given anything if he could just have said that to someone and been heard.

By the time Father Murray returned to his office Mark had gone, wended his way perilously along the city streets, now crowded with afternoon shoppers, and made his way back to the cold, empty refuge of his apartment.

Caroline

The shadows lengthened until finally the street lamps turned on to substitute their baleful light for the vigorous light of the sun, but no amount of light could dispel the gloom that had settled on Mark.

"I'm cut off," he reflected despairingly as he sat slunk down in his grimy overstuffed chair. "I can't contact anyone. If only I had never seen that weird man. If only I had never made that deal with him. What's all this money worth to me now? I want to be the way I was before."

He sat for a long time. Finally the image of Caroline came to his mind, and slowly the thought took shape that maybe Caroline could help. But how could she help? All of his attempts to speak to people had been futile, and probably it would be equally futile to try to speak to Caroline. Father Murray could see nothing he had written on the paper. No one could see or hear him, and if he went to Caroline and tried to contact her and could not, the pain would be so awful that he wondered if he could bear it. And yet as the crocus pushes its way resolutely upward in the spring through the still cold, resisting earth, so the thought of going to Caroline kept pushing its way into Mark's mind.

An hour later he was standing outside her apartment. He could see a thin line of light underneath the door and hear the sound of a stereo playing music inside. Hopefully he rang the bell, but no one came. He knocked on the door, but no one inside stirred to open it. Then he remembered that because he was invisible he was unable to make any sound; she didn't answer the door because she couldn't hear him knock. Despair gripped him again, until suddenly he remembered that he had a key to her apartment. That awful evening when he had been told that their relationship was over she had not thought to ask for the return of the key. But would the key work? Since his knock could not be heard, perhaps the key wouldn't function. Still he had to try.

Mark slipped the key in the lock and gingerly turned it. To his surprise the lock slid back and the door eased open. Evidently he could make an effect on his physical surroundings, but he could not make an effect on other people. Aware that Caroline would be frightened if she saw the door opening apparently all by itself, Mark opened it gently, peering inside to see if she was in the living room. She was not. Mark stepped into the living room and shut the door behind him. He looked around for Caroline and caught a glimpse of her through the door that led into the kitchen. He realized that she must have come home late from work and was preparing dinner.

Mark entered the kitchen and stood just inside the doorway. The room was small but cozy, simple but neatly and cleverly decorated, painted in warm colors, with handsome copper-bottomed pans hanging on the wall. A cuckoo clock, the kind the clever Germans make in the Black Forest, presided over the stove, and a kitchen witch perched cheerily on top of the refrigerator where she could keep an eye on her domain. But most of all, there was Caroline, dressed as smartly as ever, as warm and colorful as the kitchen she had decorated, but also clearly exhausted from her day at the office. She reminded him of a classy sailing ship that had sailed out to sea shining and sparkling, but now, returned from an arduous voyage, looked ragged and in need of renewal. But tired or not, here in her own kitchen she looked at home, as though this was, at least for now, where she belonged. So in spite of the haggard look on her face and her rumpled brown hair, she had never looked so desirable to Mark, and he felt himself bursting with longing for her.

"She's killing herself working like that," he reflected. "She needs a man to take care of her. She's too valuable to be wasted typing someone else's letters."

Mark pondered these thoughts with a twinge of bitterness, knowing that he might have been that man to her, but wasn't because he was always expecting her to care for him. Small wonder she couldn't marry me, he thought. He would have been one more drain on her strength. And yet here he was again with all of his needs. Should he even try to contact her? Even if he succeeded would he not become simply an enormous burden to her? But she was his last chance, and Mark hoped that she still had enough love for him that she would want him to try.

Mark approached Caroline as she stood at the kitchen counter making a salad and touched her gently on the shoulder. But Caroline continued as before; she showed no sign of any awareness of his presence. He looked for a piece of paper. He would try writing to her as he had to Father Murray in the desperate hope that somehow she would be able to read the message. There was paper on her desk in the living room. Mark sat there and carefully wrote:

> Caroline! It's me, Mark, and I am here. I know you can't see me, but, believe me, it's true. If you can read this, let me know by looking up and speaking. Unless you do, I'm without hope.
>
> Mark

Mark returned to the kitchen and waited until Caroline turned to take the salad to the breakfast table for her solitary meal. Then he placed the paper on the kitchen counter and stood back.

Caroline returned to the counter and Mark watched her as she saw the paper and registered surprise. "How did this get here?" he heard her murmur. "How strange. I could have sworn it wasn't here a moment ago. I must be more tired than I realize." Then she crumpled up the paper and threw it away.

Mark's heart turned to lead and in his despair he blurted out, "Caroline, Caroline! Look around! Can't you see? It's me, Mark. I'm here, Caroline, standing in the doorway."

Caroline wheeled around and stared uncomprehendingly at the doorway. "Mark!" she cried. "Mark! Where are you?"

Amazement and relief poured over Mark like the waters over Niagara Falls. She could hear him! She was looking right at him—not seeing him, looking through him, he knew—but she had heard. No one else had been able to see him or hear him, but Caroline could hear him!

"Caroline, I'm here. Standing right here in the kitchen with you. Caroline, you can't see me, but it's me, Mark."

"Mark, you're here? But I don't see anything. I don't understand!"

"I'm here, Caroline. I'll explain. Listen carefully. Two nights ago a strange man followed me to my apartment. . . ."

"Oh no! I'm going mad!" Caroline cried out, plunging her head into her hands. "I shouldn't have rejected him. I shouldn't have turned him away. I knew I loved him, and yet I turned him away. And now I am mad!"

"No, Caroline, you're not mad. Don't torment yourself. You were right to do what you did. I was being a child to you, a demanding child, but now I'm sorry, for I've gotten myself into a terrible mess. Listen to me now. Be quiet and listen and try to believe." And Mark reached out his hand to comfort Caroline but, of course, she felt nothing.

"No, no!" Caroline cried out, again plunging her pretty face into her hands, her long brown hair falling around her head as though it were trying to shield her from the dreadful sound. "His voice—I keep hearing his voice!"

Mark could hardly bear to look at her. He wondered if he would drive her mad. But he had to make her understand, so he kept talking, making his voice sound as low and calm as possible.

"Don't be frightened, Caroline. Try not to be afraid. Trust what you hear. Sit there at the table and listen to what I have to say."

Caroline walked slowly to the kitchen table and sat down. Slowly, carefully, Mark told his tale. Caroline listened in stunned silence to the voice speaking from the air, her face half-crazy with fear, then mingled with grief as Mark finished his story. At last he was through and the kitchen fell silent.

Caroline spoke as though to herself. "I must believe. Either I am completely mad or I must believe. No, I don't think I'm crazy. I'm here. This is my kitchen. Today is Thursday. I smell the chicken cooking in the oven. I see the salad I just prepared. I'm not mad. The voice is Mark's voice. I must believe that Mark is with me." Then, in a stronger voice, she added, "Mark, dear Mark. Is it you? Are you really here? Talk again, Mark, if you are real, and tell me how I can help you."

"Caroline, you've already helped me. You have no idea what agony it has been for me the last two days. To be thrown about on the street because people can't see you. To be unable to talk to anyone. To be transparent to people, like glass. To be like a soul without a body. You've no idea how wonderful it is that I can talk, and you can hear me."

Caroline was beginning to recover from her shock. She stood up and faced the voice and smoothed back her rumpled hair.

"Why is it that I can hear you when others can't?" she asked.

Mark answered out of what was, to Caroline, empty air. "I don't know. I don't understand it either."

There was silence for a while. Then Caroline spoke again. "Where do we go from here? What can we do?"

"I don't know that either. I had no plan when I came here except one last desperate hope that I could reach you though I couldn't reach anyone else. But I don't know what to do now."

Suddenly Mark began to sob uncontrollably, his emotions pouring out like the ocean through a hole in the dike. He struggled to stop. He *wouldn't* cry like a child to his mother.

"I won't cry, Caroline, I won't. I didn't come to cry on your shoulder, but to try to help myself. You've already helped me a lot. Now I'll go. I can't torment your life like this. It's my terrible problem that I brought on myself, and not yours. Thank you, Caroline. . . ."

"Mark! You can't go! It would be terrible for me if you left, not knowing where you were, what was happening to you. I couldn't stand it. No, Mark, stay. It's all right, stay! We'll think of something. Here, sit at the table with me. You must be ravenous. At least we can eat something together."

Mark allowed himself to be persuaded and sat at the table, feeling strengthened by Caroline's warm concern. Caroline brought the food she had been warming in the oven and prepared two places at the table, feeling both foolish and fearful as she did so. But if there were any lingering doubts in her mind that Mark was really with her, even though invisible, they vanished as they ate together. For as soon as Mark took the fork in his hand it disappeared, and when he ate the food from the plate the food disappeared too. Caroline could only watch in awe, saying to herself over and over, "It really is so. It really is so."

As Mark ate he felt better. Almost in spite of himself he commented with wry humor, "If anyone listened in on us now, Caroline, they'd be sure you had lost your mind, talking to an empty chair, and serving dinner to the empty air."

Caroline managed a smile too. "No, they'd think they were losing their minds if they could hear your voice as I can, but not see you."

When they had finished eating Caroline began to question Mark carefully, and Mark told her more about his misadventures on the city streets, his futile attempt to contact Father Murray, and his increasingly desperate feelings. Then Caroline asked him again about his encounter with the unknown man and his peculiar wife, and Mark told once more of that fateful evening. Caroline wanted to know everything the man had said, and Mark repeated it all word for word as well as he could remember. Finally he came to the part about the agreement he and the man had made. He felt guilty, and he waited for Caroline to rebuke him for his shallow motives in selling his shadow.

But Caroline offered no rebuke. She simply asked, "And how did you know he would honor his agreement?"

Mark then spoke of the contract, how he had been required to sign it in blood, and how the strange man had not signed it and had never offered him his name.

"But there *was* a written contract," Caroline said, cheering up. "Where's the contract now? Maybe it will give us a clue, some hint of what we can do."

"How?"

"Don't you see? There's only one person who can help you—the strange man himself. We must find him, and the contract is the only clue we have that might lead us to him."

"Caroline—I think maybe you're on to something. It's a long shot, but maybe, just maybe, there's some hope. That is, if we can find him."

Minutes later they were on their way to Mark's apartment, this time Mark being guided by Caroline who ran interference for him on the streets. It was not long until the groaning door of Mark's apartment gave way again to the key and Caroline and Mark stood inside. There, on the table where he had left it, was the contract.

A Bargain Is a Bargain

Mark and Caroline huddled over the document like alchemists examining an ancient text.

"The writing is barely legible," Caroline observed.

Mark rose and moved the lamp over to the table so that its light shone directly on the pages of the contract, leaving the rest of the room in eerie darkness.

"You know," Caroline said, "it's weird when you get up like that and move away. I didn't know you were gone until I heard the sound you made when you got back into your chair and I saw the lamp on the table."

"And other people wouldn't know that I was here at all," Mark observed ruefully. He peered at the document through a magnifying glass he had located amid the chaos of his desk drawer. "Here's the page that describes our agreement. I didn't read it before. There seemed no point, since he had already come up with the money. I can't make out many words. Have to assume it's just as he said, but here's the last page, where I signed. See my name in blood? He insisted it had to be that way."

"But, as you said," Caroline interjected, "he didn't sign."

"No. He said it wasn't necessary, that *he* always kept his word. I was sure careless, wasn't I? I wanted that money so badly, to make an impression on you."

"But what's this?" Caroline pointed to some faint marks on the bottom of the page.

Mark scrutinized them through the magnifying glass. "I can barely make it out. It's an address I think. Yes—50 Apple Street. And look, I think there's a name under it."

"What a strange address. It doesn't sound like any street in the city I ever heard of. What about the name?"

"Well, here is the word 'Lucas,' written right above the address. 'Lucas'—is that the man's name? Is it his first name or his last name? And why does he have only one name and not a first and last name like the rest of us? If that is, in fact, his name."

"Well, let's call him that anyway."

"I'll look up the address in my street atlas."

Mark went over to his desk again, but as far as Caroline was concerned she didn't know where he was until she saw the desk drawer had been opened. Soon Mark returned and they examined the atlas together. They found Apple Street listed in the street index and turned to the page where it was supposed to be, but for a long time they couldn't find it.

Finally Mark cried out, "Here it is!" They

peered at the tiny lines on the map and there was one small line marked Apple Street. It was no more than half a block long, on the outskirts of a remote warehouse section of the city.

"Not a very likely place for an office," Mark said, "but this must be where he hangs out. We've got to try to find him there."

"First thing in the morning," Caroline said. And Mark agreed, for it would be unlikely the strange man would be at work that late in the evening. That night they slept fitfully in Mark's apartment.

In the morning it took more than an hour for the taxi driver to find Apple Street. "Never heard of it," the driver had grumbled, but finally, with Caroline guiding him, the driver drove through an area that seemed all warehouses and bleak concrete buildings, rounded the corner, and came to a tiny street just as it was shown on the map.

"There's no sign, but this has to be it," Caroline mumbled to Mark.

"What's that?" the driver asked. "Did you say something to me?"

"Oh no, nothing, I was just thinking out loud. Here, this must be the street I'm looking for. What do I owe you?"

Caroline tipped the driver generously and asked him to wait. She and Mark started up the street, which was curiously deserted; apparently the warehouses that lined it were not used much.

"Look at that drab building at the end of the street," Caroline said. "Maybe that's it."

"Has all the beauty of a railroad boxcar," Mark replied.

They neared the building. "There's no sign on it," Caroline said, "but the door is ajar."

"There's an old man in overalls with a broom in his hand. Must be the janitor. Ask him."

"Excuse me, sir," Caroline said politely to the old man. "We are looking for a man—no, a couple really. I'm not sure of his name, but the address is 50 Apple Street."

The overall-clad man waved with his broom and said grumpily, "Door's open. Go in and look for yourself."

They entered the building. A bleak corridor greeted them; closed nameless doors ran down either side. Feeling strangely apprehensive, they walked down the bare, wooden hall.

"Wish that old man had at least given us a clue," Mark said anxiously. "I'll try a few of these doors."

Mark knocked at several doors, but there was no reply. Then he remembered. "Say, Caroline, you'd better knock. If someone is inside they can't hear my knock."

Caroline knocked, but there was only silence. "No one seems to be inside these rooms."

"I'll try the doors," Mark said. "Damn. They all seem to be locked."

They reached the end of the corridor, and Mark exclaimed, "Hey, look! Here's a door with a sign over it—50 Apple Street. This is it!"

Caroline knocked. Once, twice, three times she rapped at the door, and the third time the door swung open and Mark and Caroline were startled to find themselves looking into the expressionless face of the drab little woman.

44

"We heard you coming," she mumbled. Mark was aware that this was the first time he had heard her speak.

She stepped aside so that Mark and Caroline could enter the room. But for a long minute Mark hung back. Did he really want to go inside and meet that dreadful man again? He began to feel as he had when he last saw him, as though his will was being swept away by some strange power.

But there was no other choice, and Mark entered, Caroline walking fearfully a half-step behind him. He looked around. There were only a few windows, and the room was dark except in the center where a single, bare light bulb glared down from above them. And in that light, seated at a large wooden desk that faced the door, was the man who had taken Mark's shadow.

His stocky, powerful frame overflowed the stiff little wooden chair on which he was sitting. His rumpled suit clung carelessly to his muscular body, and his shaggy hair matched his unkempt clothing. But most striking were his dark eyes, which were peering at them intently from underneath his hedgerow eyebrows. To Mark and Caroline they seemed to have the power to see through their clothing and skin and into their very souls.

"Well," the man said in his rough voice, "I see you found me. You want something."

At the sound of his voice Mark's remaining will-power seemed to dissolve. Then he braced himself. "I've got to resist him!" he thought. Slowly he felt his courage returning, and at last he could speak.

"You can see me then?" Mark asked.

"Of course I can see you."

"But others can't." Mark was feeling stronger now.

"I see things other people can't see."

"Then she can see me too?" Mark asked, waving his hand in the direction of the man's wife.

"She can see you too. What do you want—you and your friend you brought with you?"

The man's voice was hard, and his eyes so steely, that Mark found himself floundering again as he began to introduce Caroline, feeling like a boy who tries to remember his mother's training in manners. But the man waved his hand as though to brush aside an annoying insect. "Don't bother," he said disparagingly. "I know who she is. Without her you would never have come here."

Caroline had been silent, overcome by the magnetism of the man and the awesome power that seemed to emanate from him. Now she spoke up to him with feminine courage. "Sir, we do want something. You have deceived and cheated my friend. You knew what would happen to him when he signed the agreement with you. Look, we have brought the contract . . ."

Mark found his strength again and interrupted, "And now I want my shadow back!"

The man gave a short raucous laugh, stood up, and walked around in front of the desk until he was only a few feet from Mark and Caroline. His woman, Mark noted, had disappeared. It seemed she was always doing that. The man spoke: "Don't bother me with the contract. I know what it says. Young wom-

46

an, I did not deceive your boy here. Everything that I told him was true. If he had asked me more questions I would have answered them. He made his bargain and now he must live with it. As for the shadow, I haven't any idea where he is."

The man looked at them in stony silence.

"I see," Mark said. "What should I call you? Is your name Lucas?"

The man scowled. "Call me what you will. My name is no business of yours."

"It is my business to know people's names when I deal with them."

"You should have thought of that before."

"Well I think of it now. And since you won't tell me who you are I'll tell you—you're a son of a bitch, and may God damn your soul to hell."

The man laughed uproariously.

Mark couldn't remember what was said after that. He and Caroline talked some more. They pleaded and questioned, but the man only sneered at them, seeming to enjoy their plight, playing with them the way a cat plays with a mouse. It was finally clear that there was no use talking to him anymore; he wasn't going to help.

"Come on, Caroline, we might as well go," Mark said. Then he added comfortingly when he saw that Caroline was beginning to cry, "Look, there'll be another way. We'll find another way somehow, and without his help." They left and heard the man slam the door to his office behind them.

They walked down the bare corridor in silence.

47

As they neared the entrance to the building Caroline said, "Weren't you afraid of him, Mark? I was so afraid when you called him a son of a bitch."

"I was so afraid at first, Caroline, that I could hardly speak. My will power got limp like a dishrag, the way it was the night he first came. But somehow, from somewhere, I felt some strength come to me. When I swore at him it came from anger. I guess my anger overcame my fear, and I forgot to be afraid."

They reached the main door of the building where the man in overalls had been, but he was nowhere to be seen. They started to walk slowly back to the waiting taxi when Caroline felt a touch on her shoulder. Startled, she turned to see the man's wife standing just behind her as though she had just appeared from around the corner of the building.

The little woman spoke, "You want to find him, don't you?"

Caroline was too surprised to speak but she nodded numbly.

The woman continued, "And *he*"—motioning with her hand toward the room where they had left the unknown man—"will tell you nothing?"

Caroline nodded again.

Mark had also turned in surprise at the sound of the woman's voice. Now he spoke up, "I don't know what you want or where you came from, little lady, but you seem helpful, and you seem to know things we need to know."

"Oh yes," she answered sprightly, "I know many things. Like why this woman can hear you when others can't."

"Really? Tell me!"

"Guess," she said coyly.

"Oh for Christ's sake!" Mark exclaimed.

"Oh do try a guess," Caroline said.

Mark thought a minute. Then an inspiration came to him. "Perhaps she can hear me because she loves me."

The woman clapped her hands in delight.

Mark continued. "But how about other people? Isn't there anyone else who loves me?"

The woman just shook her head.

Mark looked at Caroline. "Then you *do* love me, Caroline."

Caroline answered, "Of course I do, Mark. I told you that. I love you, but I don't see how I can live with you."

"But here you are, helping me now."

"Well, of course. What else could I do? And I *do* love you, Mark."

"But you're the only one. Well, I can understand that."

Then, turning back to the little woman, he asked, "We are grateful that you are willing to help. Tell us, then—where is my missing shadow?"

"He's not here," she answered. "The man spoke the truth about that. Neither he nor I know where he is, but he might have told you more than he did."

"But you have something to tell us?" Mark persisted.

"I will tell what I know only in a riddle," she said with a teasing tone in her voice.

"You'll only speak in a riddle?" Mark said in disgust.

Caroline said gently, "Please tell us your riddle."

The little woman looked at Caroline and Mark almost playfully and then recited like a child in school:

What's of the light,
Is always bright.
What's of the shade,
Of dark is made.

What's of the night,
In light is sight;
Black as a spade,
See where it's made.

Then, with a flounce of her baggy dress, she left them and disappeared around the corner of the building.

"What a weird lady," Mark said as he watched her disappear. Then he slowly repeated the words he had heard: "*What's of the night, In light is sight; Black as a spade, See where it's made.* Caroline, it means nothing to me. She's only playing with us."

"Perhaps," Caroline replied. "It would seem so. Yet there was something about her . . . At any rate, your shadow must be somewhere in this city. She didn't deny that. Neither did the man. Mark, we must look. We must find him."

Minutes later the taxi was pushing its way back through the streets with its two occupants—one seen, the other unseen. The search had begun.

The Search

Caroline had directed the taxi driver to take them to Mark's apartment. "We've got to make a plan," Mark said as they climbed the stairs.

Inside, Mark made coffee and as they drank it together they talked about what to do next.

"It's not just every day that people go looking for their shadows," Mark said. "Are there any experts we could ask about how to go about it?"

"Mark, this is no time to be funny. Now think—where should we begin to look?"

"Well, let's think where we would go if we were a missing shadow."

"I haven't even the slightest idea."

Mark reflected. "Well, I suppose *my* shadow might go to some place where we used to be together—some place that would be familiar to him."

Caroline thought that was the best idea they could come up with. "Let's go then," she urged.

They went to the bars Mark used to frequent. They explored out-of-the-way back streets Mark had used for short cuts and where a missing shadow might have taken refuge. Mark even pried open the lids of trash cans in back alleys he used to pass by to see if his shadow might be inside. They visited an apartment Mark used to live in. Caroline stayed out on the street and Mark waited until the present resident opened the door to leave, then slipped inside, unseen, of course, and looked around. But for all their looking, all they found was sore feet for Caroline, and more bruises for Mark, who was jostled about in spite of Caroline's able interference. By the time darkness began to settle over the city they were ready to give up, and soon they were back in Mark's apartment, weary and discouraged.

That night they slept a fitful, exhausted sleep, but at dawn Caroline was up and in the tiny kitchen putting together some breakfast.

"I'm not hungry," Mark said.

"You've got to eat to keep up your strength," Caroline protested. And then, as they sat down to their meager breakfast of cereal and toast, she added, "Where can we look today? We've been everywhere."

Mark began to look sheepish, though of course Caroline couldn't see that. "Caroline, I don't know how to tell you this, but there's one more place where he might be, one more place we used to go together."

"Yes?"

"Well—it's over on 42nd Street."

There was a shocked silence.

"Surely you don't mean 42nd Street near Eighth Avenue?"

"Well, yes, in fact I do."

"That's the red light district! Do you go there?"

"Never since I've been going with you, Caroline. Never then! You must understand."

Caroline didn't understand, and the trip to the street with the strange signs in front of dingy store fronts, and gaudily dressed women standing in doorways, was passed in pained silence. When they arrived Caroline said angrily, "You can look inside these places for yourself."

Invisible as he was, that was not hard for Mark to do. In and out of this tawdry place and that he went, but there was no sign of his missing shadow.

"You mean you actually used to go to *all* these places?" Caroline asked when Mark returned from searching the twelfth lady-of-fortune parlor.

"No, Caroline, honest to God, not all of them. But as long as we are here I thought I should look in every one I could."

At last Mark finished.

"I hope that's the last one," Caroline said. "I've been propositioned six times just standing around here waiting for you."

"You're a good looking girl, Caroline. Maybe you missed your calling!" Mark ventured the joke, speaking with what Caroline would have perceived to be a cunning, boyish grin if she could have seen him.

For a moment the pathetic humor of their situation burst over them the way a wave breaks on the shore, and they laughed, and in that laugh they felt close to each other again.

"You know," Mark said. "This search may be impossible. How does one go about finding a missing

53

shadow? And in a city like this with millions of people, it's like trying to find a *Playboy* magazine in a monastery."

They sat down despondently on a park bench, Mark sitting on the very end and Caroline close to him to discourage others from sitting on what they thought was empty space but in fact landing on Mark, for he had not forgotten the female dreadnought who had almost squashed him. They were silent for a long time. Caroline was watching the birds hopping around on the lawn looking here and there for worms and seeds. At last she spoke.

"Look at those birds. *They're* finding what they're looking for. Surely we can too. What about that riddle the funny woman told us?"

"Big help she was with her riddle."

"But maybe she was a help. Only I can't remember how it went."

"Oh I remember it all right. I memorized it."

Caroline looked at Mark in surprise. "You mean you thought to memorize it?"

"Sure did. What did you think I was doing while we were riding in the taxi back from the strange man's place? I couldn't talk to you, you know, not with the driver thinking you were having a conversation with empty air."

"Then say it out loud, Mark. Maybe something will occur to us about what it means."

Mark stood up and playfully mimicked the drab little lady,

What's of the light,
Is always bright.

54

What's of the shade,
Of dark is made

What's of the night,
In light is sight.
Black as a spade
See where it's made.

There was silence for a moment. Then Caroline burst out, "Don't you see? We've been looking in the wrong places. 'Black as a spade, See where it's made.' Now what is black as a spade?"

"My shadow I suppose."

"And where is your shadow made?"

"Made? What do you mean where is it made?"

"Well, shadows appear from somewhere, you know. They exist only when there are certain conditions."

Mark reflected. "Well, I suppose the shadow is made in the light. Yes, of course. If you stand in the darkness there is no shadow, but if you stand in the light, then the shadow appears."

"And if that's so, we have been looking in the wrong places. We've been searching in dark places, like bars, alleys, an old apartment, and," she added in disgust, "whorehouses."

Mark ignored the reproach. "Then are you saying that we've got to look in light places? But what would be a light place? This park, for instance, where there is lots of sunshine?"

"That's the problem," said Caroline. "I can't think of where a light place would be. There are different kinds of light, you know—sunlight, spiritual light . . ."

"What do you mean by 'spiritual light'?" Mark queried.

"Well, such as the light the Bible talks about."

"Like John's Gospel that we hear at Christmastime maybe: 'The light was the life of men.' "

"You've got it backward, Mark. It's, 'That life was the light of men, a light that shines in the dark, a light that darkness could not overpower.' "

"That's close enough," Mark said. "I've got it, Caroline. There's one more place we can look, a place where the light is supposed to shine: a church. And what better place to start than Father Murray's church. Let's try. We've nothing to lose."

Half an hour later Caroline was paying the taxi driver and the two of them were standing in front of St. Cyprian's Church. "It doesn't look very light to me," Mark said. "Look at all that dark ivy on those old stone walls, and the narrow windows hardly let in any light at all."

"But it isn't that kind of light we're looking for," Caroline reminded him.

They entered. But it was not so easy to go through the church buildings. Father Murray must be avoided. If he saw Caroline he would ask questions, and no story Caroline could come up with would be convincing, while the true story, they both concluded, would test Father Murray's belief to the limit. Then Caroline had an idea. She went to the buxom secretary and asked for Father Murray. If he was available she would ask him some question about the possibility of renewing the wedding date. If not they would feel more free to explore. He wasn't there, and Caroline and Mark now prowled around the great building less anxiously.

Other people were there, of course. The Altar Guild was in the sanctuary, scurrying around like ants, worshiping God with their hands, but eventually they finished and left. And there was Morris, the aging sexton, who never did any work but just hung around looking officious. "Just looking for my gloves, Mr. Morris," Caroline explained. "I think I left them here in a pew somewhere. Would you like to help me look?" But Morris made an excuse and left.

"Why did you ask that old busybody to help you look for your mythical gloves?" Mark asked.

"Quickest way to get rid of him," Caroline replied. "Looking for my gloves would be work, and if it's work he wants no part of it."

Now finally they had the church to themselves. They entered the back of the nave and looked around. Gray light found its way in through ancient windows streaked with decades of the city's dust and grime. Rows of empty pews rested stiffly on the hard stone floor as though waiting to stiffen the human beings who would fill them on Sunday morning. Off to the left a side door led into a small chapel used for meditation and small weddings. Just inside the chapel they caught a glimpse of a fine old painting of the Madonna and Child, and here and there throughout the nave other religious paintings adorned the otherwise gloomy walls.

"There had better be plenty of spiritual light in here," Mark grunted, "because there isn't very much sunlight."

"Spiritual light is what the Church is all about," Caroline insisted. "Besides, look up there in the sanctuary. It's brighter up there. The windows around it are designed to cast light down on the altar."

"And look!" Mark exclaimed. "What is that I see moving around up there? It looks like some kind of form, an outline, standing in the light of the sanctuary. Could it be . . . ?"

"I see it too! Yes, a dark form, an outline. Mark, I believe it's what we're looking for."

They hurried forward, and as they approached, the dark form stopped moving and stood still facing them. It was the Shadow all right! Suddenly Mark moved slowly. His feet felt like lead. A chill of cold fear ran up and down his spine. He felt thin and transparent, and the figure he was gazing at seemed solid and strong for all of its blackness and silence. He felt as though he was in the presence of something enormously strange, a dark but divine spirit, and it seemed to him as though the very hair on the back of his neck must be standing on end.

Caroline too had slowed down; she seemed barely able to move. "It's so frightening," she whispered to Mark.

Mark took her hand. His woman's fear brought out a flicker of masculine courage in him and he was able to make himself approach the dark form.

As they drew near, the Shadow stood there, peering at them intently. The outline was that of a human being, even though it was solid black, with none of the variations of color and tans that one could see in the handsome black people. The main impression the figure gave was of solidity, inscrutable depth, and great power. But the Shadow's face was the most remarkable thing. It was dark as pitch, with only the merest suggestion of features, except for the yellow eyes that peered out from their black background like a tiger's eyes peering from the jungle at night.

"Look at those eyes," Mark whispered as they cautiously moved closer.

"Mark, I'm so afraid," Caroline whispered back.

Mark squeezed her hand, though of course she couldn't feel it.

They were about fifteen feet away when the dark form spoke. His voice was calm, deep, resounding in the empty church: "So you've finally found me."

"Then it *is* you," Mark said in awe.

"Whom did you expect?"

The Shadow's voice was not inviting, but Mark's courage was beginning to return. "And you can see me?"

"Yes, I can see you."

"We've been looking for you everywhere," Mark said, with a hint of reproach and hurt in his voice.

"And what right have you to come and trouble me? Who helped you to find me and disturb my peace?"

"The strange man's wife told us a riddle, and we guessed from that where you were."

"She and her riddles. I might have known."

Mark tried to understand the tone in which the Shadow was speaking to him. There was anger in his voice, yes, but mostly Mark sensed a great strength and certainty, as though this figure was as strong as his sturdy, oak tree-like legs that rooted him to the ground.

"You know about her riddles then?"

"I know them well. But even then you were clever to guess. More clever than I thought you were. Though I suppose it was *she* who thought of the meaning." The dark form nodded toward Caroline, and as he did so the hard gleam in his eyes seemed to Mark to soften for just a moment.

"Yes, she helped me, as did the little woman with her riddle. Without them I wouldn't have found you."

"Well, now that you have found me, what do you want?"

Mark's courage began to fail him again. He had thought that when he found his shadow it would be something ephemeral, a powerless wisp of air, not this solid and awesome being who stood in front of him challenging him. If only those yellow eyes would not fasten on him so, searching out, it seemed, the very depths of his soul.

But at last he summoned up the strength to speak. "I want us to be joined together again. You see, this way I'm invisible. No one can see me or hear me. It's a hell I can't bear any longer."

The Shadow replied, "The hell you now experience is like the hell to which you have condemned me for all these years. You kept me hidden, concealed from yourself and others. You made me invisible, even to you. Yet while you are now so thin you can hardly muster the courage to speak to me, I became stronger, even though I was the only one aware of my own existence, I and the one you call the strange man."

"You went unnoticed? But I can see you now so clearly."

"Yes, now you see me, though others can't because of my separation from you. But now you notice me because you have to."

"You sound angry."

"Yes, I am angry. But more than that, I fear for you."

"How did you become so strong?"

"My strength came from the Law. You could have had it too, but when you lost me you lost your connection to the Law."

"I don't understand what you're saying."

"No, that was the trouble. You didn't understand."

"There are many things we need to talk about, but for now let's agree to join together again. Surely you can't let me go on like this. My life isn't worth living."

"It's not so easy to rejoin what has been separated."

"But there must be a way."

"If I wanted it there might be."

"But don't we belong together?"

"We did, but you forfeited that right." The dark figure's voice was firm, objective; he was a man stating a hard fact.

"But surely you can't like your life, skulking around like this in a church all the time."

"No. I don't like my life like this, but it's as good

as it was when I was with you. Who noticed me then? What kind of life was that for me? Did you ever bother to observe that wherever you went I went right along with you?"

"Well, a guy takes those things for granted, you know. You can't blame me. I was neither better nor worse than others like me."

"The common excuse of humankind: 'I was only acting like everyone else.' The fact is you thought so little of me that you traded me for money."

"Must you bring these things up!"

"Yes. Injustices must be settled. It's the Law."

"Okay. So much for this 'Law.' You're right. I did that. I was foolish. I bitterly regret it. I respect you now, Shadow. I see what you mean to me, that without you I can't be seen, I can't be felt, I can't make love, I can't be me. Return to me and things will be different."

"With you I must go where you go, move when you move, and suffer the life that you lead. But here I am free to move about as I please. As long as I stand in the light I have form and substance. See, don't you think I look rather good?"

"It's a fact that you look good. You look solid and strong. It's strange that I never noticed you before. Now I'm very aware of what you look like."

"No. It's too late for you. You have created your own fate. I will not go back," the shadow said with an air of finality.

At this point Caroline, who had been listening attentively, interjected pleadingly, "Oh, but you must rejoin him. You must! You can't let him go on like this."

For a moment Mark thought he saw the intense gaze of the Shadow lessen again as he looked at the anguished woman. "No, Caroline," he replied, but more gently. "I am not interested in returning. Now leave. Soon old man Morris may return, and if he hears you talking to empty space like this it will go hard with you. There is no hope. Go!"

And no matter what they said, Mark and Caroline could not get him to change his mind.

The honking horns and squealing brakes and complaining engines of the afternoon traffic beat upon their ears as Mark and Caroline left the church in dejection.

"He's just stubborn," Caroline said, tears crowding through her eyes. "Just stubborn and terrible."

"He's treating me no worse than I treated him, Caroline," Mark replied with surprising detachment. "But we're not through yet. We have one more card to play."

"Really?" Caroline said hopefully.

"Yes, we can go back to 50 Apple Street and that guy Lucas again."

"That dreadful man? What good would that do?"

"Well, we *have* found the shadow. Maybe we can persuade him to help us become joined together again. He took us apart; he can put us together."

"But your shadow doesn't want to be joined with you again."

"True, but maybe Lucas can tell us how to persuade him."

"He wouldn't help us before."

"Granted, but now that we've actually found my shadow things might be different. Anyway, it's the only thing we can do. What other chance do we have? I just can't go to the police, you know, and say, 'Make my shadow join me again.' And we just can't give up."

And Caroline agreed.

Back to Apple Street

First they rested.

"Night is no time for such a mission," Mark said. "Besides he's probably not there anyway. That seems to be where he works, so no doubt he's gone home, wherever that is. We'll go in the morning, after giving him plenty of time to get to his desk."

They spent that night at Caroline's comfortable, warm apartment. Mark wanted desperately to make love to her; never had he loved Caroline as much as he did now. "But," he reflected to himself, "how can I make love to her when she can't feel me, when my body is less than a wisp of air to her? That Shadow must be made to come back to me! I can't even make love to a woman without him. To live without him is to live without love."

So he talked instead. "Caroline, you're giving me so much. You haven't gone to work since I came and asked for your help. You may get fired. Why are you doing all this for me?"

Caroline looked worried for a moment. "I did get a notice today from my boss. He wants to know where I've been. He says that if I don't explain my absence I may lose my job. But it doesn't matter, Mark. I want to help you, that's all."

They rose promptly in the morning, and they had finished their breakfast by the time the sun made its way over the tall buildings and cast a few rays of light on the imprisoned streets below. Soon they were riding in a taxi through streets already busy with rushing people, honking taxis, and clanging trucks. In a half hour they arrived at Apple Street. As Caroline paid the driver Marked whispered to her, with a flash of his old wry humor, "When there's more than one passenger in a taxi these guys expect a bigger tip. Are you sure you're paying him enough?"

"Mark! This is no time to make jokes," Caroline giggled.

"What's that you say, lady?" the taxi driver asked in a puzzled voice.

"Oh nothing, nothing at all. Sometimes I talk to myself." Then, as she and Mark walked toward the building, she said to him, "You see the trouble you get me into with your jokes?"

But by the time they saw the man in overalls, there as usual sweeping the walk, Mark's brief flight of humor had left him. This time they went past the man without speaking. They knew where they were going now and didn't want to risk another rebuff. Down the bleak hallway they went, past the closed doors on either side, and on to the end of the corridor with the mysterious door marked 50 Apple Street.

"I'll knock this time," Mark said. "If they can see and hear me, maybe they can hear my knock."

But Caroline reached out toward him. "Mark, I'm afraid. Aren't you? He's so weird."

Mark said gently, "If you're afraid, Caroline, I'll go in alone."

But Caroline wasn't about to let Mark go in alone, and she motioned to him to knock.

Mark knocked once. Nothing happened. A second time, and still no sound from within. A third time, and now the door swung open, and they faced the little woman in gray, and beyond her, seated at his desk facing the door as before, the man who had brought such evil upon them but whose help they now had to seek.

The expressionless face of the woman broke for a brief moment into an inviting and pleased smile which vanished as quickly as it came. "You are back," she whispered.

"Thanks to you," Caroline whispered in reply as they entered the room.

"You're back," said the man gruffly, like a dog growling at an intruder.

Mark felt the old chill of fear steal up his spine, but in spite of it he spoke up boldly, "Yes, we are back to tell you that in spite of you we have found my shadow."

The inhospitable expression on the man's face didn't change on hearing this news. "Someone must have helped you. You could never have done it alone."

"You don't seem surprised."

"I am not surprised. I knew you had found him. I have ways of knowing these things."

"Well, why should you be so ungracious about it then? What harm is it to you if I have found him?"

"Do you think I like to see my work undone? I work hard at my job, and it's always getting undone."

"It's only fair, now that we have found him," Mark persisted, "that you tell us how we can be rejoined.

"You have a strange idea of what's fair. You're the one who's trying to undo our agreement. But a bargain is a bargain and must be kept."

"Our bargain was the money for the shadow. I agree that a bargain is a bargain, but even a bargain can be changed if both sides agree."

"What makes you think I might agree?"

"Well, I'll return all your money to you."

"You've already spent some."

"I'll replace it."

"I don't want the money. I wouldn't have given it to you in the first place if I had wanted it. No, I have what I want. I have set your shadow free, and that is more to my liking than anything you can do for me."

"But we *have* found him," Mark said triumphantly.

"And you also found that he doesn't want to rejoin you, didn't you? So it did you no good to find him."

"But you must know a way it can be done. Surely you could persuade him if you wanted to."

The man replied, "And I don't want to. There's

no use talking further. I'll agree that you have done well so far—better than I thought. Your woman here—he gestured toward Caroline—helped you, of course. Still you must have had other help too. No matter. I give you credit for what you have done, but it's still no use. Now you might as well leave. If you do not go, I will, leaving you here alone to talk to the walls."

Caroline exploded, "You're a beast!"

"Thank you," the man said. "That is one of the nicer things people have said about me." And he rose to his feet, turned his back on them, walked to a door at the rear of the room and vanished.

Caroline and Mark were left alone in the empty room; the drab little woman had disappeared at some point during the talk. They exchanged downcast looks and then walked away from the room, slowly down the empty corridor, and out the main door of the building. They were about to return to the waiting taxi when they heard a now familiar voice behind them.

"I have another riddle, if you please."

Caroline and Mark turned around to see the little woman who had slipped up behind them from somewhere and stood looking at them coyly.

Mark was about to say something impatient when Caroline spoke up and said, as one woman speaks to another when women-matters are to be talked about, "You have another riddle for us, dear lady? We'd like very much to hear it."

"And you?" the lady asked, turning to Mark.

"Well, I'm glad you've come to speak to us again without your husband around, but I would rather you just told us outright what we need to know. Why do you tell us things only in riddles? We almost missed the meaning of the first one."

"I speak in riddles because I think in riddles. It's the only way I can think."

Mark rolled his eyes at Caroline and started to say something, but Caroline turned to the woman and said gently, "Tell us your riddle, please."

She acted greatly pleased at this invitation, stood up as tall as she could, held her hands behind her back, and spoke like a child reciting proudly in school:

> What is two,
> Yet is one,
> When an evil
> Can be undone.
>
> To make two free,
> Two must agree;
> How this is done,
> Only love can see.

"I don't have the slightest idea what it means," said Mark.

The woman looked disappointed, and exclaimed, "Why do you always have to know what everything means!"

"Well you know what it means, don't you?" Mark queried, hoping she would reveal the meaning to him.

"It's only a nice riddle, that's all. I just think up nice riddles."

"But you're trying to help us," Caroline interjected. "Doesn't he—I mean your husband—mind it when you give us riddles?"

She brightened up again: "Oh, but he doesn't know."

Caroline persisted, "He says he has ways of knowing all kinds of things. He knew that we had found the Shadow."

"But he doesn't know what I do. I'm too close to him."

Mark spoke again: "But how can you be his wife and still betray him?"

She looked shocked. "I don't betray him! He does what he must do, and I do what I must do. We don't betray each other. We each follow our own laws."

"Well," Mark said, "call it whatever you want. I don't know what your laws are, but I'm glad they're different than his laws."

Caroline again entered the conversation: "We're grateful to you for your riddle, and it *is* a nice one, but can't you give us even a hint what it means? You see, we may never understand. We almost didn't understand the first one and this one seems even more mysterious."

"Oh, but I really don't know what it means. I only know the right riddles. I never know what anything means." And with that the little woman half-skipped away like one of the little birds she resembled, leaving Mark and Caroline alone.

They glanced toward each other and then Mark spoke. "She tried to help us anyway."

"I can't help but like her, though I don't understand why she puts up with that horrible man. What do you think of her riddle?"

Mark pondered it out loud: "*What is two, yet is one, when an evil can be undone. To make two free, two must agree; how this is done, only love can see.* I don't know what to think of it. Maybe something will occur to us later. Come on. Let's hope our taxi's still waiting."

The Shadow

The taxi wasn't waiting, and Caroline and Mark had to walk several miles while looking for another. It gave them a chance to talk. Caroline ignored the people who stared at the woman talking to herself.

"We need to come up with a plan," Mark said as they walked along.

"At least we know where to find the Shadow," Caroline added.

"Yes. He's probably still at the church. But even if we find him we don't know how to persuade him to rejoin me. That guy's got a mind of his own. And Lucas was worse than no help at all."

"But we do have the woman's riddle."

"Though we don't know what it means. Still, the meaning may come to us somehow, as it did before. When you can't figure things out, sometimes clues pop into your mind from somewhere."

"But that takes time," Caroline added.

"So let's give it time," Mark said. "Let's go back to your apartment for a while and think about it.

We'll see what comes. Then in the morning we'll go back to the church and look for the Shadow again."

"Can you stand being this way for one more day—I mean, invisible?"

"Do I have a choice?"

They finally found a taxi that seemed to have strayed and lost its way into this part of the city. The driver was surprised when a lone woman hailed him. "You shouldn't walk around these streets by yourself, lady," the driver said paternally. Caroline mumbled an excuse for her odd behavior, then rode in silence. Caroline and Mark didn't talk, for the driver would have thought she was talking to herself and was crazy instead of just a bit odd.

The remainder of the day Caroline and Mark discussed their situation and the mysterious riddle that seemed their only hope if the Shadow was to rejoin Mark, but they came up with nothing. At last they fell into an exhausted sleep. When the gray dawn lighted the streets the next morning they were already up. Caroline cooked some eggs, Mark made coffee, and they sat down to breakfast.

Suddenly Mark leaped up from his chair excitedly. "The riddle," he exlaimed. "I think I have it."

Caroline's face brightened.

"Look. The first part is easy enough: *What is two yet is one.* That clearly refers to me and my Shadow, for we are two because we are apart, but one because we belong together. *When an evil can be undone.* The evil was the unloosing of the Shadow from me."

Caroline interjected. "It started before then,

Mark. The evil started when you agreed to the bargain."

Mark accepted the rebuke. "You're right. That was the evil, but, regardless, the riddle says it *can* be undone."

"Now about the second verse; that's the hard one."

"Okay. *To make two free two must agree.* That means that the Shadow and I must agree."

"I see, but we've already found out that he doesn't agree with you on anything."

"But we've got to try again. There must be something—something on which we can agree."

"And how about the last line, *How this is done only love can see?*"

"I don't know. This line puzzles me. But let's start with what we do know—that he and I must agree upon something."

Caroline's apartment was not far from the church. After a fifteen minute walk, which was the usual harrowing experience for Mark, they were poking through the old building looking for the Shadow and hoping to avoid people who might ask unanswerable questions. Fortunately it was early enough in the morning that, although Morris the sexton had opened the church, few people were about.

They looked everywhere but the Shadow couldn't be found, and the more they looked the more nervous and desperate Mark became. Dreadful fantasies of what might be his awful fate swamped him. Suppose the Shadow had left the church? Suppose they could never find him again? How could Mark ever live out his days as an invisible person? He found himself thinking of suicide. But could he commit suicide, being transparent like this? Perhaps invisible people don't ever die—then he would live forever like a frightful ghost doomed to walk endlessly over the earth, always trying to reach out to people and never being able to do so.

Mark forcibly pulled his mind back from thoughts that were becoming more bizarre and morbid. "I must control myself," he thought. "I must not give in to these thoughts. My mind is playing tricks on me."

So they searched. They looked in the sanctuary where they had seen him before—but he wasn't there. They went through the main parish house building—but there was no sign of him. Mark even went into the office where the hearty secretary had her desk and peeked into Father Murray's office— but the Shadow was not to be seen. Then they returned to the church for one more look in the sanctuary, but still there was no sign of him. Mark's apprehension grew, and in spite of all his efforts his dreadful fantasies engulfed him again. Then as they were leaving the church Mark caught a glimpse of something moving inside the little chapel with the handsome picture of the Madonna and Child.

"I think I see him!" Mark whispered in awe.

They hurried over and entered the chapel, and there was the Shadow standing near the altar. Mark halted some fifteen feet away from his long-sought foe whom he wanted now for a friend. The desperate fears he had been having for his future were now replaced by the unearthly apprehension Mark had felt before when he stood in the presence of the dark figure. The Shadow looked at Mark as piercingly as before out of his yellow eyes, gleaming from his night-black face.

"You are back," the Shadow said as though simply announcing a fact.

Mark could hardly speak he was so afraid. He wondered if after all this search it would come to nothing because his knees felt like water and his stomach like ice. But then a trickle of strength came to him from somewhere, just as it had when he had faced Lucas, and he finally managed to say, "We are back. We have had another talk with your strange friend, the man at 50 Apple Street."

"You call him strange. He's not strange to me. But he was of no help to you, was he?"

"How do you know?"

"I know him better than you do."

"No. To be honest with you he was no help. But his wife helped. At least, she tried to."

"She's always interfering. I suppose she told you another riddle?"

"You seem to know a lot about those two." Now that they were talking Mark was beginning to feel less in awe, more in control of himself.

"We have some things in common."

"Well, I'm getting to know a lot more about them myself. You sound as though you're still angry."

"Has anything changed so that I should not be angry?"

"Yes. The woman's riddle has changed things."

"She makes sense only when she talks in riddles, for her riddles express the Law."

"What is this about the Law?"

"You don't know about it, do you? That is obvious from the way you have lived your life. It is clear that you think *you* can make up your own Law. But the riddle helps only if someone can understand it."

"Well, I think I know what the riddle says. It says that if you and I agree on something, then you must rejoin me. Do you know the riddle?—*To make two free, two must agree....*"

"Yes, I know the riddle," the Shadow interrupted, "and you are correct that if we can agree on something, the evil can be undone. But how can I possibly agree with you? I am against everything you are and against everything you have been doing with our life."

Caroline piped up. "But it does mean, then," she said adamantly, part statement, part question, "that if you and he can agree on something, you must consent to be rejoined?"

The Shadow seemed shaken, and he began to walk back and forth in agitation. "I can't deny it— though certain other conditions have to be met too. But our differences are too great. You could say that it is our very differences that made it so easy for the man to separate us in the first place."

"Like what differences?" Mark perservered.

"Like the life you lead. It's a sham. You aren't real. You pretend to like people, but you don't really. You only want to be admired by them. Everything you do is secretly done only for yourself."

What was it Mark was hearing? Was it an angry

man, full of rancor? Certainly the Shadow was angry, but it was more than that. The things he was saying were true. Mark had to admit it to himself. Yes, that was it! When he listened to the Shadow it was like seeing himself; it was like looking into a mirror and seeing his true image reflected back to him.

But now Mark became angry. Surely the Shadow had to look at some things about himself too. "But *you* don't seem to like people at all."

"Perhaps not. But when I dislike people at least I am genuine. I don't dissemble. I never pretend to be something I am not. When I say things to people I mean them; when you say things you don't mean them. You compliment people only to flatter them. You make promises you intend to keep only if it serves your purposes. You say things only to create a favorable impression of yourself."

"It sounds as though you've been watching me."

"All these years."

"But these are dark things. I think they would belong to you, who are dark, and not to me."

"You, who pretend to be light, are really dark, and I, who appear dark, am filled with light."

"Yet it's *you* who are destructive. Look at what's happening now. You are perfectly willing to destroy me, to see me invisible forever, just to suit yourself."

"That's right. And this doesn't bother me in the least."

"And you think that's not being dark and destructive?"

"It is being dark and destructive, but I'm destroying only what doesn't deserve to exist."

"You have no conscience."

"I have no conscience. I leave that to you. But I do follow the Law."

"But you're also destroying yourself. You can't tell me that you have much of a life, hanging around this church by yourself like this."

"No. As I said before, it isn't much of a life, but at least I'm on my own."

"But surely you're not happy like this?"

"No, but neither are you happy."

"I thought you were only my shadow, that is, the dark outline of my body made by the light, but now you talk of your separate existence."

"That shows how little you noticed me all these years."

Caroline now interrupted the conversation, speaking with great agitation, "There you both are, accusing each other of wrong. It seems to me that you're both wrong. Each of you hates the other, but to what purpose? Why don't you both agree to change and come together again?"

Mark added, "She's right. Let's put our differences aside and join again. I agree that much of what you say about me is true. But you must know that in these past few days I've changed. I see things differently now. If you rejoin me, our life will be different."

"There you go again," the Shadow answered. "You make a plan for union, but you have only yourself in mind. Of course you want to be visible again. For this you need me. But there's nothing in what you say for me. The woman here is right. I am evil. But you are evil too, and if I am evil it is because you make me evil. We are equally evil, but I do not care if I am destroyed in the process of destroying you. At least I'm not out to preserve my life at any cost the way you are."

"I accept your rebuke, Shadow, but I can't agree with you that either of our purposes is better served if we remain separated. It's true that much about me has been false, but not everything. I do try to build up a form to life. I try to make a fabric of things and achieve some goals, even if sometimes these goals are wrong. You, on the other hand, seem only to be interested in destroying what I try to build up, the way you are destroying my life right now. I may be wrong, but not entirely wrong, and you are not entirely right either. Now the riddle says that if we can agree, the evil of our disunion can be overcome. Surely you must agree with what I've just said."

"I don't see your point," the Shadow said, apparently honestly puzzled.

"Let me be more blunt. Can't we agree that each of us is necessary? Can't we agree that if each of us gives a little ground to the other, it might be to our mutual benefit and that on this basis we could live together again as one being?"

"We could, if I believed what you say about yourself."

"I'll make a contract. I'll promise that things will be different and sign my name to it."

"You've already made one contract and now are trying to break it."

"That's not fair and you know it. I didn't know what I was agreeing to."

"No. You were so greedy you didn't make it a point to know. You thought so little of me that you would give me away."

"And this makes you angry?"

"Yes, it makes me angry and I will not agree with you. Now, we've talked long enough. The matter is hopeless. I will not rejoin you and I don't have to, for you have not pointed out to me a ground upon which we can meet. You've gone too far to heal the breach with more words and empty promises."

Mark gave Caroline a despairing look, but since she couldn't see him he had to add in words, "Caroline, there's no point in talking further. Let's go. I can't persuade him that things can be different. We're no closer to agreeing now than we were before."

Caroline nodded, and they began to walk away slowly and solemnly, while the Shadow stood in the light cast into the chapel from the window above the altar, watching them depart.

But as they neared the chapel entrance Mark's eyes fell on the scene of the Madonna holding the Infant Jesus in her arms. He suddenly stopped and stared at the picture. "Caroline," he said, "I think maybe I have it. I think I have it. Look at that picture, Caroline. What do you see?"

"I see a picture of Mary and Jesus, of course."

"No. It's a picture of love. Remember the woman's riddle: *To make two free, two must agree; how this is done, only love can see.* So it has to do with

love. Where love can agree, then the two can become one."

"You mean," Caroline said, with wonder at
Mark's insight, "that if the Shadow and you were to
agree about something you both love, then he could
rejoin you?"

"Exactly."

"But whom can the Shadow love?"

"Whom do I love? He's right, you know. I've
used people, not loved them. I've even used you.
Yet it's also true that I *do* love you. I think you're the
only person I do love. Maybe that will save me."

"But he must love too if the reunion is to happen."

"But I think he does. Those glances he gives
you, Caroline—I think he loves you too. Come on.
Let's find out."

Mark turned and walked back toward the Shadow who was still standing where they had left him.
He was no longer afraid now. Caroline followed.
The Shadow seemed to look at them anxiously,
fiercely, longingly, all at once.

Mark said to him. "You remember that if we
agree on something, you must rejoin me?"

"So the riddle has said, and so the Law is."

"Then I would claim that there is this that we
agree on: you and I both love her." And Mark gestured triumphantly toward Caroline. "Isn't that so?"

A look of both anger and relief showed in the
Shadow's fierce eyes. "I can't deny this. I can't deny
that I love this woman. It's the only point on which
we agree. It's the only place where you are not
false."

Caroline gave a little gasp. Mark continued, "No, there's one further point. I now agree with you on much of what you've said about me. I agree with you that I've lived a sham life. You're right in this— so right that I'll promise you this: I will not make you conform to the Law of the riddle and rejoin me unless you want to."

"Mark!" Caroline cried out in horrified admiration.

The Shadow's eyes showed astonishment. "I can't believe what I'm hearing from you," he said. "I must believe you because you didn't have to say it. When you say that, I feel a change taking place in myself. I'm different than I was before."

Mark asked, "Then we agree?"

A pause. "I agree. You're correct that this life I lead alone is not satisfactory. It is better if I am joined with you, provided that you remember your change, and that you provide for me as well as for yourself. I will therefore accede to the Law of the Riddle and be rejoined. But for that we will need the help of the man and his wife."

"How so?" Mark exclaimed, dismayed.

"By a ritual he undid the thread that holds us together. By a ritual we must be united again."

"But he's ruthless. He'll not do anything to aid us. He delights in my suffering."

"He can be made to act. He's ruthless, but he too is under the Law."

"Then let's go to see him now," said Caroline.

According to the Law

A n hour later a taxi pulled up in front of 50 Apple Street and three passengers got out—one seen, two unseen. "Please wait," Caroline said to the driver as they entered the building.

Down the empty corridor they went, and when they reached the door at the end, the 50 Apple Street sign was there as usual. Three knocks and the door swung open. The little woman stood in front of them. When she saw the three of them (she had no trouble seeing the Shadow as well as Mark), she let out a little gasp of what appeared to be pleasurable surprise. She said nothing, but with a gracious wave of her arm ushered them inside.

But there was nothing gracious about Lucas who was again seated behind his big desk facing them as they entered the room. His growly face looked wilder and darker than ever, his massive body seemed possessed of even more animal energy, and he was clearly not pleased to see the Shadow. He said to Mark, "I've been cheated. Someone has cheated me. It was a fair bargain that I made, and now someone has unraveled it. How did you persuade him to come with you?"

For a moment Mark was intimidated by his ferocity, but the presence of his Shadow gave him courage and he spoke up boldly, "How it happened that he came with me is not your concern. The fact is that he has come willingly."

The man retorted, "You may have found some way to bring him with you, but he will not rejoin you."

"Do you think he would have come back here with me if he was not willing to rejoin me?"

"And what makes you think that I would rejoin the two of you even if he is willing?"

"Because of the Law," Mark answered.

"What do you know of the Law," the man replied scornfully.

"Very little. But I now know it exists, and I know the Law is greater than you are and that you are bound to serve it. And I know that the Law says you must act now to reunite that which you separated because the necessary conditions have been met."

The man scowled. "Someone has been meddling in my affairs. But you are wrong in what you say. Even if the conditions for reunion have been met I can't reunite you. I am a negative power only. I unravel, but I do not bind together. I destroy, but I never create."

Mark's face fell. Could the Shadow, who had told him of the Law, and the woman whose riddle spoke of reunion, be wrong? He looked at the Shadow helplessly.

The Shadow spoke, "What you say is true, but there is another one here who can unite what you have severed, and under the Law you must allow her to act."

The strange man turned now to the Shadow. "You, dark one, I have known of you for many years when he (motioning to Mark) didn't know you. Your tie with him was loose, so loose that I could unravel it with my spell. If the tie had been stronger, not even I could have undone the knot. So I dissolved the bond, for I am the one who unloosens what can be unloosed, and destroys what can be destroyed. That is my nature, and so I act. But you didn't complain. You came with me willingly, and preferred your lonely life to a life with him. Now you tell me that you agree to this reunion?"

"Yes, I now agree. I am forced to agree by the terms of the Law, and I am hopeful besides."

Caroline interjected, "You two seem to know a great deal about each other. All this time, while we didn't know you, Shadow, he knew you and you knew him."

"That's the way it was," the Shadow replied.

Mark spoke to the man again: "Enough of this talk. You're delaying. Now put us together again. And if you can't do it, then let your woman do it. For what other woman could my Shadow be referring to?"

The man snarled, "I've been cheated. Cheated! But I have no choice."

Then, motioning to his wife who was standing nearby, he said, "Act! Unite them!"

The woman stepped forward, but now she

didn't seem so drab and gray. Her manner had taken on a surprising decisiveness. She said nothing but motioned for Mark and his Shadow to come together, and then with her hands she placed them deftly back to back. Then slowly she moved around them in a clockwise direction twelve times, and then once counterclockwise. Mark felt something like a physical impression on his back.

Then he heard Caroline cry out: "Mark! I can see you!" Suddenly she was in his arms, weeping for happiness. She ran her hands over his shoulders, down his sides, and over his hips. She wove her fingers through his rumpled brown hair, and felt his nose, lips, and ears. She squeezed his now solid bones and stroked his muscles. And all the while she kept repeating, "See, I can feel you again. You're solid again, Mark!"

And Mark felt solid. He felt a sense of buoyancy and energy he had never known before. There was a new spring in his legs and a clearness to his mind, and as he hugged Caroline he rejoiced in the strength of the embrace he gave her, and the warmth of her body that he could feel. Then he remembered, "But where's the Shadow? He was standing right here."

Caroline pointed to the floor. "He hasn't gone. See, there he is—your dark outline on the floor. He's right where he belongs, attached to you."

They held each other for a long time. When they finally looked up they saw that the room was empty except for themselves. The man was gone, and his wife had disappeared with him. The bare bulb glared down on a barren room and an empty desk.

"While we were holding each other they must have slipped out of the room," Mark said.

"And good riddance!" Caroline said fiercely. "Except I shall miss that funny little woman."

They looked around the room half-expecting to see Lucas appear again from somewhere, scowling at them fiercely, or to be startled by the sudden appearance of his wife from some secret place. But there was only emptiness and silence. At last Mark said, "Come on. Let's get out of here and see if the taxi's still waiting."

The taxi was still there, the driver pacing impatiently back and forth beside it.

"I was just about to leave, lady," he grumbled.

"Thanks for waiting. I was delayed. You see, I had to meet my friend here."

The driver looked darkly at Mark. "This guy wasn't with you when you came. If he's going to ride back too I ought to charge you extra."

"No problem, Buddy," Mark answered. "I owe it to you many times over."

The driver looked at him strangely. Then they entered the cab and he started the engine. Soon the rattling taxi sped away.

It's So Good To See You

A week later Caroline and Mark ran jauntily up the stairs of St. Cyprian's Church for their appointment with Father Murray. "No need to slink in here this time," Caroline said as they walked boldly past the Altar Guild ladies and Mr. Morris.

The secretary greeted them with her usual buoyant enthusiasm: "Miss Cameron, how are you this morning? And Mr. McLaughlin, it's good to see you again."

"You don't know *how* good it is," Mark replied with a grin.

Not knowing exactly how to take Mark's remark, the secretary continued, "Just go right in. Father Murray is expecting you."

Father Murray greeted them warmly. "Caroline, so good to see you. And Mark, let me shake your hand. Where have you been lately anyway?"

"Oh, let's just say that I've been around. But I'm back now—to stay, I hope—and Caroline and I are here to ask you to make plans again for our wedding."

"If that's what the young lady wants, then that's what we'll do!"

It didn't take long to make arrangements for the wedding; they were the same as before except that the date was different. Soon Mark and Caroline were out on the busy street again. A bustling man carrying a briefcase and umbrella bumped into Mark, and turning to him, annoyed, said, "Hey, Buddy. Can't you watch where you're going?"

"Oh thank you," Mark replied. "Thank you for bumping into me like that and saying 'Watch where you're going!' "

The man gave Mark a puzzled look and hurried away muttering to himself, "Strange bird. The people in this city get more weird every day."

Mark waved at passing taxis, but they all acted as though they had more urgent business and passed them by. At last he let out a bellow—"Taxi!"—and a cab stopped. "Mister," the driver said, "that's the loudest voice I've heard in a year. Where'd you learn to bray like that?"

"These guys are sure rude nowadays," Caroline muttered.

But Mark didn't mind. "Thanks," he said, as they got in the car. "That's one of the nicest things I've ever heard anyone say to me. I'm so glad you could hear me bray like a donkey."

The driver rolled his eyes as though to say, "Good God, what kind of a guy is this?" and started the taxi down the street. Mark and Caroline were soon talking.

"You went through a lot for me, Caroline," Mark said. "You even got fired from your job."

"It doesn't matter. I can get another job."

"Right. And tomorrow I start my job. My classes are all in the evening now, so it will work out. There's not much pay, but it will see us through for a while. It's strange, though, what happened to Lucas' money, isn't it?"

"Yes, very strange. When we returned to your apartment it was gone."

"I know it was on the table when I last left."

"Mysterious."

"It would have been pretty nice if it had still been there, but it wasn't mine in the first place. I do wonder what happened to it."

"They left us in that bare room, you know. Maybe they slipped out quickly so they could come back here and get the money."

"Perhaps. Lucas seemed to have mysterious ways of getting in and out of my apartment. The truth is, there are a lot of things about him that we don't know. What does he do? What's his business? Why does he have such a funny little woman for a wife? There are so many unanswered questions."

An inspiration came to Mark. "Caroline, look where we are. We're not too far from Apple Street. Let's go back there one more time. Perhaps we can get some answers."

Caroline gave him a horrified look. "Oh, Mark, why go back to that dreadful place? Something awful might happen."

"What can happen? The awful thing has already happened."

"But I'm afraid. Why must you go?"

"I guess I have to find out everything I can. But you don't have to come with me. I'll send you home in the taxi if you like, and I'll walk to Apple Street. I don't want you to go if you're afraid."

Caroline was afraid, but she didn't want to be left behind, and soon the taxi arrived at 50 Apple Street. They asked the driver to wait and walked together up to the front of the building where the strange man had his office.

There was the bare looking building just as before, and there by the door was the janitor with his broom. They ignored him, though Mark noted as they passed that he seemed to give them a quick, curious glance. They went again down the empty corridor with the locked doors on either side until they reached the end and the door that led into Lucas' office. They looked for the sign over the door.

"Look!" Mark said, "the 50 Apple Street sign is gone!"

"How strange," Caroline said.

Mark knocked the usual three knocks, but no one opened the door. He knocked one more time; nothing happened. He turned the knob and the door swung open. They stepped gingerly inside. The desk and chair were there as before, but otherwise the room was bare.

"How peculiar," Caroline said. "If I didn't know better I'd say this room hadn't been used for months."

"It looks so empty," Mark said. He went over to the desk. "I want to find out what kind of damned business that man is up to." He pulled out the drawers one by one. "Look. They're all empty. There's not a thing in them—not so much as a scrap of paper."

"And look at the dust on top of the desk. It looks as though it hasn't been cleaned for a century. Was it here before?"

"I can't say. I had other things on my mind and would never have noticed."

Mark's eyes roamed about the room. "Not a clue," he said.

"Then we'll never know more about him?" Caroline asked.

"I guess not. Except—well—let's ask the janitor. Maybe he can tell us something."

They reached the front of the building again and there was the man sweeping the walk. "Excuse me, sir," Mark said politely. "Would you mind answering a question for me?"

The man grunted his agreement.

"The large man who occupied the office at the end of the hall—the man with the little woman who dressed in the gray, baglike dress. Can you tell me where they've gone?"

The man leaned on his broom and stared at them. Then he said in his heavy voice: "The room at the end of the hall's been empty for six months. All the rooms in the building's been empty. Building's for sale. No one comes here anymore, except me to look after the place."

Caroline interjected, "No, you must have misunderstood. We mean the room at the very end. The room that had the sign over it '50 Apple Street.' "

"Weren't no sign over no door," the man said.

"But surely you know that someone was there. You do remember my coming and going a few times, don't you?"

"I remember you. I wondered what you were up to, but it wasn't no business of mine so long as you weren't up to no mischief."

"But you must have seen someone there," Mark said.

"Mister, like I said, ain't nobody been here except me. Can't tell you nothing more, and I've got work to do." Then the man shuffled off.

Mark and Caroline looked at each other in disbelief. There was a long silence. Then Mark spoke, "Are we crazy, Caroline?"

"No, we're not crazy."

"Was it all a dream then, some kind of nightmare?"

"It was no dream. I have the letter from my boss firing me to prove it."

"Then I don't understand."

"I don't either. But maybe it doesn't matter that we don't understand."

"What matters then?"

"What matters is that as you stand there in the light of the sun you can look at the ground and see your shadow. What matters is that I can see you as well as hear you. What matters is that others can see you too."

"You're right. But there's one more thing."

"What's that?"

"That we're here together. Come on. To hell with that damned Lucas. Let's get out of here before that taxi driver loses patience and leaves without us."

In a few minutes the taxi was on its way back to the heart of the city, leaving Apple Street far behind.